I Found My Father in a Women's Prison

The Journey Begins

Tracey Brown, Ph.D.

Also by Casa de Snapdragon

A Scattering of Imperfections
Katrina K Guarascio

The Poetry Café
John Newlin

Harriet Murphy – A Little Bit of Something
Janet k. Brennan

A Dance in the Woods
Janet K. Brennan

Recollections of an Old Mind, West
Janet K. Brennan

*Visit **http://www.casadesnapdragon.com** for details on
these books and others.*

I Found My Father in a Women's Prison

The Journey Begins

Tracey Brown, Ph.D.

Published by Casa de Snapdragon Publishing

All names of inmates in this book have been changed to protect their identities and privacy.

Library of Congress Control Number: 2007939239
ISBN 13: 978-0-9793075-3-9

Published by
Casa de Snapdragon Publishing Company
12901 Bryce Avenue, NE
Albuquerque, NM 87112
http://www.casadesnapdragon.com

Printed in the United States of America

TABLE OF CONTENTS

INTRODUCTION

On November 11, 2003, I looked out of my living room window to see two unmarked police cars pulling into the driveway along with a very distinctly marked Bossier Parish Sheriff's Deputy car. I knew they were there for me because of events of the previous week. Actually it began over a year ago when I met a certain female.

It would be nearly impossible to explain what circumstances brought me to be in this situation without mentioning the name of the female that brought the charges and everything that she did to "enhance" her position to make sure I remained here as long as possible.

I won't use her real name for several reasons, mainly because of my fear of reprisal against my family and myself. As you read my story you will fully understand exactly what I mean, so I'll just refer to her as "Ms. X".

I had met Ms. X through a mutual friend. She owned a nightclub. I started going once or twice a week, not for the drinking, but for the companionship of others. I had recently lost my best friend of 20 plus years and found a certain level of comfort when I was at the bar. Ms. X and I became friends and eventually I was helping at the bar as bar back and later bartender. I learned that Ms. X had done several consulting jobs as an "efficiency expert" along with a great many other colorful jobs she'd held over the years.

When the bar closed in December of 2002, Ms. X and I were given the opportunity to consult together for the owner of a local motel who was having some problems with his employees and his clientele. We learned through that experience that we worked well together. When Ms. X learned that I was interested in opening a sign shop, she suggested that I do so in Haughton because there wasn't anything like it in the area. She also suggested that I move myself and my 12-year-old daughter out there. She claimed the schools were the best around.

So, in February of 2003, Kira and I moved to a small trailer in Haughton and opened our sign shop. Ms. X and I decided to make it a partnership. She would bring in the business with her contacts and I would do the actual sign work. My big mistake was to let her use her existing company name and incorporation without having any additional paperwork drawn up. She said that using the existing incorporation would allow us to "go out of business" if things didn't work out and neither of us would be held liable.

Several months passed and we were barely making it. I had moved myself and my youngest daughter into a home that belonged to a friend of Ms. X. She was in the market to sell and I thought it would be the right move at the time. Since it had 4 bedrooms, I asked my oldest daughter, her boyfriend, and my grandson to come and live with us. Little did I realize that everything that I did would culminate into the biggest mistake I'd ever make in my life not only affecting me but all those around me.

Ms. X and I decided to move our offices to an existing building owned by Ms. X. To remodel the building Ms. X took out a credit card in the business' name. She gave it to me to use for the business since cash flow was limited. Several months later when the bill arrived, she realized that she hadn't signed for it as a business card but with a personal guarantee on the card. That is when things started their downward spiral.

I was offered the opportunity to pay the bill off or she would see that I went to jail. She wasn't going to be responsible even though most of the charges were business expenses. She had also had me order 5 computers so that we could teach computer classes, but would later deny any knowledge of them even though she had admitted to others that she had authorized it.

One vital fact of importance that I have failed to mention was Ms. X's late husband had been Chief of Police in Bossier City and knew almost every policeman, sheriff's deputy and judge in the parish.

Little did I know as I watched the detectives walk up my drive that my fate was sealed and I was about to begin a journey that not only would affect the rest of my life, but the rest of my eternity.

As I suspected I was arrested for "identify theft" and was taken to the Bossier Parish Jail. Fully confident that I could prove my innocence and that this was only going to be a minor inconvenience, the reality of the situation took several days to sink in.

I spent the next five months waiting in a pre-trial dormitory in Richland Parish Detention Center. This was followed by another two months in Bossier Sheriff Correctional Facility. I would soon learn that I was to spend my next ten months incarcerated and I would forever be labeled a convicted felon with a record.

During those seventeen months I lost not only my freedom, but every possession I owned. My mother would have no contact with me, my father died, and my own brother would join forces with Ms. X to make sure I was locked up for as long as possible.

But in spite of all that I lost, possessions, family, and friends, I found something far greater than anyone could imagine. I found my Father in that women's prison. The following pages take you on my expedition into a world of faith and love that I wouldn't trade for anything this world has to offer.

PART I
THE JOURNEY BEGINS

DAY #1   MY ARREST

"You have the right to remain silent. Anything you say, can and will be used against you in a court of law. You have the right to have an attorney present during questioning. If you cannot afford an attorney, one will be appointed to you, free of charge, if you wish. If you decide to answer questions now without an attorney present, you will still have the right to stop answering at any time until you talk to an attorney."

How many times have you heard those words on TV and movies? Somehow they take on a whole new meaning when a sheriff's deputy is reciting them to you.

Sheriff's Detective T. C. Bloxom of the Bossier Parish Sheriff's detective's office read those words to me at 11:00 on the morning of Tuesday, November 11th, 2003.

What I thought could be cleared up by a little rhetoric, turned out to be the beginning of one of the most fascinating, heart-breaking, and eye-opening experiences of my life; an experience that would change my life, forever.

My arrest and the next 523 days turned out to be the best thing that ever happened to me because it started me on a journey to find and build a wonderful relationship with my Father.

I went through the normal booking procedure that I'd seen so many times on TV of being photographed and fingerprinted at the Bossier Parish Jail. After that I was issued my meager necessary items for health and sanitation. Then I received the customary red and white stripe uniform. For bedding I was given a thin, white blanket and a beat up plastic mattress before I was ushered into a six-bed cell.

For the first time in my life I felt totally alone, lost and bewildered. Fortunately there were a couple of other females in the cell that explained what would happen. They told me that I would be arraigned within the next seventy-two hours and bail would be set by the judge. I don't remember much more about that day except crawling into my bunk, covering my head with that skimpy blanket and crying myself to sleep.

DAY #2   THE LEGAL PROCESS

After breakfast this morning, one of the guards came and told me I was to be downstairs in the courtroom within a few minutes. Finally, the judge would hear my side of the story and let me go home. That was not to be the case

As I stood in front of the judge the charges were read. My mind was swimming so fast that I didn't really hear them. He never asked if I was guilty or innocent. All he asked was, "Can you afford an attorney?" I don't know how I kept down what little food was left on my stomach, as I said, "No, sir."

As he closed my file, he simply instructed the IDB (Indigent Defender Board) to be my attorney and set my bond at $50,000.

My whole body shook in terror. This wasn't the way it was suppose to be. When was someone going to listen to me? When did I get my chance to speak? The guard escorted me back to my cell. Once again I retreated into the solitude of my bunk while I blocked out everything that was going on around me.

Day #3   Cell Description

Mere words on paper cannot truly capture the essence of a jail, especially an old, outdated, dirty holding facility that should have been evacuated and closed years before. The drab, dank, colorless walls, the sharp clang of metal locking into metal, the pungent smell of fear along with the incessant drip of a broken shower only intensified the feelings of hopelessness that I felt for my future and myself.

In the rusty metal locker beneath my bed I found an old blue Bible. The pages were flimsy but remarkably intact. The gold writing on the front of the hard blue cover identified it as Gideon Bible. I asked one of the female officers who's Bible it was and she snapped back, "Yours, if you want it."

I now had something besides sleep to occupy my time, something familiar and hopefully, comforting.

DAY #7   TRANSFER TO RPDC

On Monday morning, white plastic bags were brought in by the female guard on duty and we were told to pack our possessions and bring our bedding outside of the cell. The only possession I had to claim was my Bible. It wasn't near as fancy as the Bibles I had at home. Christ's words weren't in red and the print was very small but it was mine and I was taking it with me.

Three other females and I were handcuffed and taken downstairs where we were allowed to put on our street clothes. Within an hour we were in a navy blue van headed east to Rayville, Louisiana. In Bossier Parish, if you can't make bail, you are shipped there while you waited for your court dates. We arrived at Richland Parish Detention Center about 5:30 in the evening, after a two hour drive.

Guards and trustees scurried about as we were individually shown into a small bathroom where we showered and deloused. During processing I was issued the customary two bras, two pairs of panties, one towel (formerly used), one set of very thin sheets, and two pairs of new socks with a mesh bag to be used in laundry. Then I had my picture taken for my all-important ID badge that would be necessary to eat, go to the library and in general, everything!   I was also handed a stack of badly copied pages that contained all the rules and regulations of the facility.

I was told to drop my mattress and belongings in Lockdown Cell #6 because the "pre-trial" dorm was full. This is where I would spend my first few nights; in this six by eight room with one set of metal bunk beds, one sink and toilet combination. That was it!

All of the other inmates had eaten, so my fellow travelers and I ate our first meal of beans, greens and cornbread. After supper, I was allowed to "rec" in Dorm C, the pre-trial dorm. I sat down by the door and watched as these women scurried about as if they didn't know my whole world had just come crashing down.

Around ten pm we were returned to our lockdown cells; lights out at 10:30. There were two other inmates in the cell but I chose to ignore them and once again draw into my own world.

The cell was so quiet that I could hear the faint sounds of jail doors slamming and locking in the adjacent corridor. I tossed and turned for what seemed like an eternity but no matter how I tried to sleep, something kept me awake. I finally reached down on the floor beside my bunk and picked up my Bible.

I was no stranger to the Bible. I was raised in the Southern Baptist Church and my parents made sure that I attended Sunday school, Training Union, GA's and every other training opportunity the church offered. I accepted Christ when I was seven years old and proceeded to live what I thought was a good, normal Christian life. So, the Bible and its promises were not alien to me. I soon learned to do something that I had never done before and that was to claim its magnificent promises.

There were two other things the Holy Spirit showed me that night. The first was that with all of the arguing that I had done with myself, even though I knew all about God, I didn't truly know Him as Master of my life. That night we met on a different level. I surrendered all that I knew about myself to all that I knew about Him. I knew that was a commitment I had to make before I could find His will for my life, even in this place.

The second truth I was about to be taught was that God had a purpose for my being there. For some reason I felt compelled to open to the book of Job. Maybe it was because it was always Daddy's favorite book or maybe it was because I felt camaraderie with Job and the trials he had to face. Whatever the reason, the first verse my eyes scanned through the dim light of that cell was Job 1:19; "I alone survived to tell you…"

God was showing me through this messenger to Job that I wasn't placed in jail for something I had done but for what I *could* do. I promised God that night that I wouldn't take a single step without conferring with Him, first, and that I would document every step of my journey so that others might learn from my experience.

I got on my knees and asked God to let me learn from this time that I had to spend there and let me learn how to become closer to Him and walk closer by His side. It was at that point I started my odyssey toward finding my Father. It's a decision I wish I had made years before. The course of my life was re-set and I was changed forever.

DAY #9   THE EVENING PRAYER

About eight o'clock tonight I was called to the window and told to get my mattress from lockdown. I was being moved into C dorm, bunk #74. One inmate graciously, or out of self-defense, gave me a comb and deodorant. That night I had to shower with seventy-four other women. There were six showerheads, but we were totally exposed to the prying eyes of the entire dorm. There was one girl in there that set her chair up by the shower to watch her girlfriend while she was in there.

I was forced to use my panties as a washcloth and state soap as shampoo since washcloths and shampoo weren't state issued items. I had nothing to sleep in, so I had to put on the same uniform that I had worn for two days while others were putting their uniforms and towels in the laundry basket to be washed during the night.

I made a futile attempt at watching the small television set in front of the dorm. There were no chairs so we all were forced to sit on the cold, concrete floor and crane our necks upward. There was no use trying to listen to what was coming from the TV due to the incessant noise from my fellow dorm mates. I finally resorted to reading the closed captioning as best I could.

I was glad when the announcement of *lights out* came over the intercom. Finally, I would be able to rest my ears from the cacophony of sounds that they had been exposed to all evening long.

My bunk was just a short step away from the back door, all the way across the dorm from the interlock window. When the lights went out, the room was still illuminated by two or three overhead lights so the guards could keep watch over their charges. Once lights go out there is to be no talking or movement of any kind, except necessary potty trips. I pulled the blanket over my head to try and block out the light that was almost directly overhead. I started to pray and ask God for His protection because I was alone and scared. The silence was broken by a lone voice coming from the front of the dorm:

"Dear Lord, hear our prayers and forgive our sins." Then in unison the rest of the ladies repeated the same line. I listened as the responsive prayer continued.

Let us keep the faith and let us all be friends.
As I talk to you from behind these walls
Locks, chains and security guards.
Our love for You will keep us strong.
Keep us safe, dear Lord, until we all go home.
May the Lord watch between you and I
While we're apart
One from another.
In this we ask
In Jesus name.
Much prayer – much power.
Little prayer – little power.
No prayer – no power.
We don't have any problems
All we have is faith in God.
I said, we don't have any problems
All we have is faith in God.
When life's problems come your way
Lift your hands up high and say
Hallelujah, Hallelujah, Hallelujah
Jesus loves you and so do I.
Who's the Father (Leader)
Our Father (Response)
Who's the Father (Leader – a little louder)
Our Father (Response)

Who's the Father (Leader – a little louder)
Our Father (Response)

Silence fell over the dorm. I started to hear slight murmurings, ever so softly. I strained to hear what was being said. It was the Lord's Prayer. Each lady was quietly repeating the prayer to herself. After an appropriate amount of time to finish the prayer, another voice came from the back of the room as she led the second part of the responsive prayer.

If I should fall down
Like I sometimes will.
If I can look up
I can get up.
I am
Somebody
I am
Somebody
I am
God's child
The me I see
Is the me I be
Today I see
A better me.
I am
Somebody
I am
Somebody
I am
God's child
Walk with me, oh, Lord, I pray
Keep me safe throughout the day.
Take my problems, big and small.

Lift me up when I tend to fall.
Not my will.
But God's will be done.
In Jesus name.
Amen.

Total silence then fell over the entire room. I fell asleep, confident in the knowledge and peace that God was watching over me and no harm was going to come to me, now or in the future because I was in His hands.

This prayer was written by several former inmates and had been repeated every night since the prison opened in 1996. It was a tradition, a wonderful tradition in which I was happy to participate.

Day #10   Protection Psalms

I called home and learned that my family was still being persecuted by Ms. X. Her longing for revenge against me was extending to the ones I love the most. Her vengeance did not seem to know any bounds, legally or illegally. As a mother I felt completely frustrated over not being able to protect my children and grandchild.

Not knowing where to turn, I walked over to one of the ladies that I knew spent a lot of time reading her Bible. In utter frustration I asked her, "When is she (Ms. X) ever going to stop?"

Monica told me to read Psalm 91 and Psalm 25 as protection Psalms. She told me to not only read them, but commit them to my heart so that I could call upon them when I needed them. I went back to my bunk and read both Psalms

Psalm 25

A Psalm of David. Unto Thee, O LORD, do I lift up my soul.
O my God, in Thee have I trusted,
  let me not be ashamed;
  let not mine enemies triumph over me.
Yea, none that wait for Thee shall be ashamed;
  they shall be ashamed that deal treacherously without cause.
Show me Thy ways, O LORD;
  teach me Thy paths.
Guide me in Thy truth, and teach me;
  for Thou art the God of my salvation;
  for Thee do I wait all the day.
Remember, O LORD, Thy compassions and Thy mercies;
  for they have been from of old.
Remember not the sins of my youth, nor my transgressions;

*according to Thy mercy remember Thou me, for Thy goodness'
sake, O LORD.*
Good and upright is the LORD;
   therefore doth He instruct sinners in the way.
He guideth The humble in justice;
   and He teacheth the humble His way.
All the paths of the LORD are mercy
     and truth unto such as keep His covenant and His
testimonies.
For Thy name's sake, O LORD,
   pardon mine iniquity, for it is great.
What man is he that feareth the LORD?
   him will He instruct in the way that He should choose.
His soul shall abide in prosperity;
   and his seed shall inherit the land.
The counsel of the LORD is with them that fear Him;
   and His covenant, to make them know it.
Mine eyes are ever toward the LORD;
   for He will bring forth my feet out of the net.
Turn Thee unto me, and be gracious unto me;
   for I am solitary and afflicted.
The troubles of my heart are enlarged;
   O bring Thou me out of my distresses.
See mine affliction and my travail;
   and forgive all my sins.
Consider how many are mine enemies,
   and the cruel hatred wherewith they hate me.
O keep my soul, and deliver me;
   let me not be ashamed, for I have taken refuge in Thee.
Let integrity and uprightness preserve me,
   because I wait for Thee.
Redeem Israel, O God,
   out of all his troubles.

Tracey Brown

Psalm 91

We live within the shadow of the Almighty,
 sheltered by the God who is above all gods.
This I declare, that He alone is my refuge, my place of safety;
 He is my God, and I am trusting him.
 For He rescues you from every trap
and protects you from the fatal plague.
 He will shield you with His wings!
 They will shelter you.
His faithful promises are your armor.
Now you don't need to be afraid of the dark any more,
 nor fear the dangers of the day;
 nor dread the plagues of darkness,
 nor disasters in the morning.
Though a thousand fall at my side,
 though ten thousand are dying around me,
 the evil will not touch me.
I will see how the wicked are punished,
but I will not share it.
 For Jehovah is my refuge!
 I choose the God above all gods to shelter me.
 How then can evil overtake me or any plague come near?
For He orders His angels to protect you wherever you go.
 They will steady you with their hands
to keep you from stumbling against the rocks on the trail.
You can safely meet a lion or step on poisonous snakes,
 yes, even trample them beneath your feet!
For the Lord says, "Because he loves Me,
I will rescue him;
I will make him great because he trusts in My name.
When he calls on Me, I will answer;
I will be with him in trouble
and rescue him and honor him.

I will satisfy him with a full life
and give him My salvation."

David, in these Psalms, made me see that I could only do one thing to save my own sanity and that was to turn my family over to God. He was the only one that could protect them in my absence.

My evening prayer: *"Oh, Lord, when does this storm end? I lay here tonight trying to figure out what lessons you want me to learn.*

I know that I have been praying to you every day but somehow by putting my words to You on paper seem to make things more real, and a little easier to understand.

Your love and power continue to amaze me and, in spite of all the pain I must go through, I am grateful to have personally witness how Your love will always overcome evil each and every time.

As You told Jehosophat in II Chronicles, "The battle is not yours, it is the Lord's."

DAY #11   LITTLE SLIPS OF PAPER

I was making up my bed this morning and found a small slip of folded yellow paper with a scripture on it. I asked my bunkmate about it. She said that was my "daily blessing." It seemed that a couple of the girls write out the scriptures and randomly put them on the beds each morning.

One of the inmates "managed" for me a T-shirt, a jump suit, and some sleeping shorts. Finally, I was able to have my uniform washed after my shower tonight.

When I spoke with Chris, he said that he and his Dad had gone to my house to get our things, but a deputy, Ms. X and the landlady showed up and told him they couldn't get anything. The landlady claimed it was all hers and the deputy took her side. After a great deal of talking, they did get the baby's things and some of their things. I did not know what would become of my stuff but I imagined that it was all lost to me for now and forever.

As I laid in my bunk that night, a virtual movie of all my possessions ran through my mind. The strangest part of it was that the items that came to mind were not the big items like my computers and business equipment that I had worked years to acquire, but little items that most people would consider insignificant. There was the angel statue that Catherine and Kira had given me for Mother's day; photographs of the girls as they grew up; my collection of carousel horses that had been given to me over the years to mark special occasions. All this was gone.

All I could do was lay there and pray: "Lord, I guess this is another hurdle You and I will have to face, together."

DAY #12   DON'T JUDGE THOSE AROUND

Daily Blessing - *Matthew 7 1-2. "Judge not least ye be judged."*

I have now had a few days to survey my surroundings more fully. Much of what we think we know about prison and prison life is based on television and motion picture portrayals. Unfortunately the media still tends to exploit the most tasteless, graphic or shocking aspects of imprisonment and distort the true nature of life behind bars.

When I was escorted into C Dorm, I was surprised I couldn't tell a murderer from a bogus check writer. They were all just women. Now, I'm just one of them. I know I can't look at what they've done and judge them. I have to look just at whom they are now and what God can do with their lives.

I am finding that God is using so many ways to speak to me now that I am opening myself up to Him, more and more. It seems He always directs me to the right person when I need guidance and now is using tiny slips of paper or just points me to the right scripture. He is such a wondrous God!

DAY #13   COMMUNION

Daily Blessing - *Proverbs 3:5-6 "Trust in the Lord with all thine heart and lean not to thine own understanding, but in all thy ways acknowledge Me and I will direct thy paths"*

This morning's breakfast was two small hot cakes, one greasy sausage, sliced in half and a carton of milk.

I laid down for my morning nap at 7:30, only to be awakened an hour later when Communion was announced over the intercom. It had been a while since I had taken Communion, so I decided to go. I discovered that a layman from a church in Rayville came almost every Sunday to offer Communion. Our dorm might not always get to go, depending on who was the supervisor on that particular shift, but I vowed to go whenever it was offered.

We had a young girl come in today. She was charged with shoplifting at Wal-Mart. I learned that she was not only hiding items in her clothes but she was also cramming things in her three-year-old son's pants

Tina, who was in on her second DWI charge, said she knew this girl on the outside and that Tina's son use to baby-sit the girl's two young children so that she could go to the "dope man."

I'm starting to really get an idea of how far some people will sink to obtain what they want. As far as this group of women was concerned, it was usually drugs or what they could sell or trade for drugs.

I played several hands of Skip-Bo to keep my mind off the fact there were no visitors coming to see me, even though it was visitation day.

DAY #14   LOSS OF CONTROL

Within a few days of incarceration, I begin to fall into the power of the jail. The realization of separation from an outside world, detachment and acceptance of these circumstances brings about a prisoner's sense of peace. This is a strange peace in a world where time has no meaning and no responsibilities or pressures. You are now in a position with no sense of duty, no demands, nothing that must be done except the mindless and automatic routines of daily survival. We exist beyond people's reality, other people's truths are on the other side of these walls.

One of the hardest, deflating realizations we must all face is that whatever goes on beyond the locks and walls is totally out of our control. We are prisoners who must rely on people outside to help with the details of daily living – from buying clothes, food, and presents for children, to phoning lawyers, agencies, and officials who don't accept collect calls.

My evening prayer: "Father, despite this feeling of powerlessness I thank you for the assurance that there is one thing I can do – PRAY!"

DAY #15   MS. JO'S BOYS

The first night that I was in the dorm I noticed a group of four women playing cards by the wall next to the phones. One of the ladies called me over to tell me that I had caused her heart to skip a beat the night I came in. She went on to tell me that when I was called to the window, they called me by my legal name, Evelyn Brown. She said that her heart went into her throat as she looked toward the door because that was her sister's name and she knew there would be no way her sister would be in jail. We both had a good laugh over that incident and manage to develop a friendship from it.

Ms. Jo also reminded me of a very special lady in my life, Alice B. Alice B was a housekeeper we had when I was growing up. She was a precious, God-fearing lady. Alice B. taught me a lot and I loved her dearly. Maybe it was this recollection that caused our friendship to develop so quickly but I soon learned that Ms. Jo also had her own special relationship with the Lord.

One morning, while she was sharing a cup of her "special recipe" coffee, she told me a story I will never forget. Ms. Jo told me that when her two sons were young she moved them to one of their uncles in the country so they would be safe from the gangs and trouble in the city.

Several days later she was sitting on the front porch, crying because she missed them so much. She said that God spoke to her as plainly as "we are talking now." He told her or rather asked her "Why she wasn't willing to trust her sons to His care, after He gave His Son for her?" She said that she put herself in her car and drove as fast as she could to get them and bring them home.

She told me this after she learned that one of these boys (now men) had taken an overdose while in jail himself.

Andre had just learned that he had been sentenced to 16 years for manslaughter and attempted murder. She said that he was firing back to defend himself and a stray bullet went through a wall of a nightclub and killed a girl. Someone later told her that the shot that killed the girl came from inside the nightclub but the Indigent Defender didn't care to look into it.

Ms. Jo was in on charges of shoplifting in Monroe and was waiting for extradition to Atlanta, Georgia after the outcome of the Monroe sentencing.

DAY #17   EVE OF THANKSGIVING LETTER

Daily Blessing: *Ephesians 5:20 "Giving thanks always for all things unto God and the Father in the name of our Lord Jesus Christ"*

Today is Thanksgiving. I haven't heard from Mother since I was arrested. I remember her last words to me on the phone; "Well I guess we'll just have to pray about it." Despite my letters and attempted phone calls there has been no contact. I will use my letter to her as my entry for today.

Dear Mama,

I lay here tonight on the eve of Thanksgiving, 2003. The room is relatively still and quiet. Two overhead lights illuminate the large dorm room with just enough light for the guards to watch over us from the interlock. As I face the reality of spending the first Thanksgiving away from my family and friends on the outside, the Lord is showing me that I have, without a doubt, more to be thankful for this year than ever before.

That might sound like a trite statement said by so many this time of year but just how many of them are in jail knowing they won't see their family or possibly not even talk to them on Thanksgiving.

I have lost so much in the last 16 days; my freedom, my home, all of my worldly possessions, most of my family, but I have gained so much more.

God has given me the insight to see that I haven't lost my family, but found a greater appreciation for the ones in my family that really count because they care and have stuck by me during this trying time and I know they will be there through this whole process.

I have been privileged to have received a very minute perspective of how God must have felt when Christ was falsely arrested and the pain that Christ's separation during His time on earth must have torn at the heart of God. I know this because of what my own daughter's imprisonment has done to me, all because she was my daughter and chose to stand by me and for that reason alone she was persecuted.

Satan and those who work for him know that the quickest way to break a mother's heart is through her children.

Ms. X's vengeance and hatred toward me has caused her to strike out at my children. That is one thing the Lord is really opening my eyes to; the effects of hatred upon a human being. Had I not found a new relationship with my Heavenly Father I could easily be caught up in the same web of detestation.

I'll have to admit that shortly after I was arrested I was so filled with hatred that I laid awake at night trying to think of ways I could retaliate. Then one morning I opened my Bible to Matthew 5:44 "Love your enemies, bless them that curse you, do good to them that hate you and pray for them which despitefully use you, and persecute you." I knew the Lord was speaking directly to me and that what I must do is put as much effort in praying for her as I had been putting in hating her. Only then would I be able to find peace and I have.

Your loving daughter
Tracey

DAY #18   SUPPORTING YOUR HABIT

One of the first survival tips I was introduced to was "rolling cigarettes." This is a must, even if you have never acquired the nasty habit of smoking. It is a way to "earn commissary" from those individuals too lazy or just too uncoordinated to roll their own.

Unlike most of the ladies in here I had never been introduced to the art of "hand-rolling" since I had never tried marijuana, so I learned to roll using an old ball point pen and the wrapper from the rolling papers. This was also an economic decision; a box of tobacco, which yielded 36-44 cigarettes, was $1.35 as opposed to a pack of 20 cigarettes for $2.75 or a pack of Newport's at $4.75. My budget was approximately $20 - $25 a week (and lucky to get that), so every penny had to be conserved. This even included saving butts and in times of desperation smoking "re-rolls."

Then there were those of us who became skillful enough to roll with a filter. The filters came from an occasional "splurge" in the budget by ordering a pack of "real" cigarettes.

Another method of supporting your habit was to "work" for others. This included a multitude of duties from hand laundry to assigned duties like dorm cleanup. Dorm cleanup was something that each one of us had to do once a month. Two bunks at a time were assigned to sweep and mop the entire dorm plus clean the toilets, mirrors and shower that morning and evening. Lonnie paid me some cigarettes to do her clean up for her today. It's ironic that this was always something that I had someone else to do. I wouldn't clean up my own bathroom but now I'm cleaning up after 75 women.

The real skill of acquiring cigarettes came, I must admit, from those that couldn't afford even a box of tobacco, or spent their money on snacks and learned the dubious art of "begging."

Another form of survival, when it came to smoking, was *never smoke after anyone else and always holds your cigarette when giving someone else a light.* Never, ever, let anyone hold your cigarette. You don't know where their hands had been and most times you don't want to know. The numerous bugs and illnesses such as Hepatitis and TB floating around surely were worse than the cancer threat you were exposing yourself to with the cigarette.

DAY #20   LOSS OF POSSESSIONS ON THE OUTSIDE

Daily Blessing – Philippians 3:8 " *I count all things but loss for the excellence of the knowledge of Christ Jesus, my Lord, for whom I have suffered the loss of all things; and do count them but dung, that I may win Christ."*

The reality finally hit me today that I had actually lost everything I'd ever owned; everything I had ever worked for, been given, treasured was gone. No one is going to be able to help me get it back. The Holy Spirit kept telling me over and over that the only thing I could do was "Pray it through."

Once again I opened my Bible to Job. There it was in Job 42:10: "And the LORD turned the captivity of Job, when he prayed for his friends: also the LORD gave Job twice as much as he had before."

All this time I had been praying for myself and ignoring all the misery and pain around me. I was ignoring the new found "friends" to whom God had sent me to minister to.

As I started praying for each of them and their particular problems and situations God finally gave me a peace that only He could give over losing things on the outside.

My evening prayer: "Lord, even though I have lost everything I owned, please don't ever let me forget that with You I have more than enough to start over."

DAY #22   THE FIRST OF MANY

We had our first DOC move out today. When an inmate is finally sentenced, they become property of the Department of Corrections or the state and the parish no longer funds them. DOC and parish prisoners aren't supposed to be in the same population (or allowed to have any contact) with each other. If a DOC and a parish prisoner should get into a fight it causes a great deal of problems and paperwork. There were four ladies that were moved to other dorms. I hadn't gotten to know any of them very well but I saw the emotions that were exhibited in the friends that they had made.

There were three prisoners, we learned, going home within the next few days. I had come to know all of them quite well. So well in fact that I knew what they would be doing as soon as they got out. They would go right back to the drugs that put them here and on the road to their own self-destruction.

The Lord put a burning desire in my heart to commit to paper what I was feeling in the form of a poem. Other than a few short poems I had written for my Mother years ago, I was not experienced in writing poetry.

As I picked up the pencil and the pad of paper, the words seemed to flow as if they were being whispered in my ear, straight to my heart. I wrote the poem and put it on the bed of my bunkmate and closest ally, Valerie.

It didn't take long for the tears to form in her eyes and roll down her cheek as she read it. I wondered if I had hit a nerve. Perhaps it hit too close to home for her to be objective.

All she said was, "God has given you a great talent, Tracey. Use it for Him." I had been praying so hard for the

Lord to show me just what He wanted of me. Could this be the way I was to reach out to these women?

I went to bed praying, "Lord, here I am, your servant. Use me."

THE EVE OF SELF DESTRUCTION

Their time is almost finished
Their race is nearly won.
What lies ahead for those dear souls
Once they walk into the sun?

Once they talked of better days to come
When drugs no longer ruled their life.
Are they headed for sweet victory
Or a continued life of strife?

The eve of self destruction
Is currently at hand.
No more putting off a decision
It's time to make a stand.

What causes us to take the path
We know we mustn't choose.
Is it momentary satisfaction
Or an inner decision to lose.

Momentary satisfaction comes
And goes so very fast.
Only God in His wisdom
Gives the kind that will last.

On the eve of self-destruction
Before you leave this place
Let God choose your direction
And the decision you must face.

Let Him lead you down the road.
With His divine instruction
Toward a life of "victory years"
Not the day of self-destruction.

DAY #23   BROKEN WATCH

Early this morning I was awakened and told I would be going to court. This meant another two hour trip to Benton. Maybe I would finally see my lawyer and clear things up.

When we arrived in Benton, we were put back in the same cell where I had spent my first few days of incarceration. The jailhouse lawyers back in Rayville had already briefed me on what would happen.

Right before I went in to the courtroom, a female in a two-piece business suit called my name and told me that she would be representing me. She said I was to be arraigned and the only thing I was to do was answer, "not guilty," when the judge asked me "guilty or not guilty?" I tried to discuss my case with her but she said she had no time and we'd get to it later. I did as I was told and returned to my cell. Unfortunately, it was so late, by the time the judge finished with all the arraignments from Rayville, we had to spend the night.

When I was shackled at RPDC, the handcuffs broke the stem to my watch. I see now that the Lord was using this to make me take a different look at time. It is a resource. Moreover, it is a unique resource. *It cannot be accumulated like money or stockpiled like raw materials. We are forced to spend it, whether we choose to or not, and at a fixed rate of 60 seconds every minute, 60 minutes an hour, 24 hours a day. It cannot be turned on and off like a machine or replaced like a human. It is irretrievable. It is a resource I should not and could not waste.* I have no idea how long I will be here, but I need to be a good steward of my time and study His Word so I would be prepared to do whatever God had planned for me.

I looked around and found myself back where I started, but something was missing. I didn't have my Bible. I didn't have my source of comfort that helped me get to sleep at night. The Holy Spirit soon reassured me that even though I didn't have the book, I had the Author.

I drifted off to sleep while praising and thanking God for being with me no matter where I was.

DAY #24 FIRST COMMISSARY

Whenever an inmate spends the night away from RPDC they must face the same humiliation that they face when they are initially brought into the facility; the de-lousing shower. This is especially true if you are coming from Bossier Parish because several inmates that had been transported from Bossier Parish were lice invested and that is one of the greatest dreads of any prison.

I was so glad to get back to my now familiar faces and surroundings. Another perk in coming back was that I had made my first commissary. It was like Christmas. No longer would I have to beg and borrow cigarettes, snacks or coffee. I had my own, thanks to a good friend on the outside.

An essential part of prison life is being allowed to make commissary. Unfortunately, there are women that will hit other people up pretending like she has been broke for awhile and ask for a handout of necessities or stamps. When you inquire what she did with her money, she'll use some lame excuse such as that she only had a couple of dollars or owed it all to medical, which automatically deducted it from her books.

Most inmates that try this game are quickly discovered and labeled as a "roach." But there are gullible inmates just like there are suckers a plenty in the free world that will give her what she asked for, even when the proof was obvious that she had money. She had simply chosen to spend hers on cigarettes or gambling debts. These inmates will try to spend other people's money on what they really need.

Since I was one of these suckers in the free world, I was quickly tagged as an easy mark. Thank God for my good friend, Valerie. She just silently stood by me, arms akimbo, as I unpacked my bags and neatly arranged the contents in my drawer. She didn't have to say a word. Her demeanor was such that everyone in the dorm knew to leave my treasures and me alone.

DAY #25   CRYSTAL'S LETTER

Tonight turned out to be quite an emotional and heart wrenching experience. Crystal brought a letter to Valerie and me to ask if she could read it. She said that she had done a lot of thinking about all of the pain and heartache that she had brought to her ex-husband and their two young daughters. She was in on drug charges and it wasn't her first time. There seemed to be a long line of skirmishes with the law and incarcerations. In desperation, her method to raise money she needed to support her habit included writing checks against her ex-husband's account.

Tears flowed freely down her cheeks as she read all the wrongs that she had done to her husband and her children and mostly to herself. She begged for his forgiveness and asked for another chance.

Her words were so compelling that every one of us that were gathered around could actually feel her pain. One by one some of the others began to tell their stories and how their lives of addiction had destroyed their lives and left a permanent imprint on their children.

One of the stories that really grabbed me was Valerie's. She told of how she left her two sons, then two and four, because she didn't want to change her life of drug abuse but she also didn't want to drag her sons through it. As a mother, I couldn't fathom anything that would cause me to make a decision to leave my children like that. I still had a lot to learn about the overwhelming hold that drugs could have on someone.

My prayer that evening was, *"Lord, please give me the capacity to feel each of these ladies pain, the strength to be able to cope with it, along with the wisdom to know what You'd have me do with it."*

Once again the Holy Spirit led me to write another poem, especially for Crystal and her precious daughters.

PARTY LINE TO HEAVEN

Hello my darling daughters.
I'm so sorry I'm not there
To play to games you love to play
Or brush and braid your hair.

When you slip under the covers
And go to bed tonight,
Mommy won't be there to tuck you in
'Cause Mommy did something that wasn't right.

You see, Mommy has a problem
You never really knew.
At times you saw a different Mommy
The one that always yelled at you.

You are so very small.
I wish I could explain.
But all I seem to ever do
Is cause you heartache and pain.

I love you more than life itself,
Always know that this is true.
But one day I tried some drugs
That came between me and you.

Drugs are those horrible monsters
You talk about in school.
They destroy your life in many ways.
Drugs are never "really cool."

Mommy will get well soon
And leave those drugs alone.
With God's help, my darling girls
I'll soon be coming home.

Tonight and every night
When you go to bed at seven
Pray for Mommy and I'll pray for you
On our own party line to Heaven.

DAY #26   MS SANDY

Today was another DOC move out. This time I knew someone in the group, Ms. Sandy.

Society's war on drug has created a whole new category of drug criminals - the elderly and previously law abiding who are drawn to low level drug dealing in order to make ends meet. These new drug criminals are drawn to the drug trade because the selling of these illegal substances has become so lucrative that almost anyone can be tempted into breaking the law -- even past-their-crime-prime senior citizens.

I met such a woman in Ms. Sandy. Ms. Sandy had been busted for selling crack to an undercover cop. Ms. Sandy ran her own game of survival in jail. There was no one to regularly send her money and the little she did receive on occasion had to go to her medications. She met her needs by "lending" cigarettes, coffee or whatever anyone needed for a price. That price was usually, two for one, or three for one. Even though this was completely against regulations and she could have gotten lockdown time for her business practices, she did what she had to do in order to survive. I don't know why she liked me, but she only charged me one for one when I needed anything

When she left, she left all everyone who owed her anything and she would have to start all over in another dorm. After she left, one of the girls from her hometown told me an amusing, yet sad story that would always cause me to remember Ms. Sandy. Amber told me that it was not unusual to see Ms. Sandy riding her Hov-a-round down the road to go to get her drugs from the "dope man," or making her deliveries.

DAY #31   LEAVING AN EMPTY EXAMPLE

Daily Blessing – *Matthew 5:16. "Let your light so shine that others will see Jesus in you."*

Tina went home today, after serving her parish time of thirty days. She left me a note, along with a partial package of hot chocolate. Later that night after showers, I stood in line at the water cooler to get my cup of hot water to enjoy the hot chocolate left behind for me. After a twenty minute wait, my cup was filled and I headed back to my bunk to enjoy my warming cup of chocolate. As I opened the package to empty the contents, I found it to be empty. I wasn't able to be mad or disappointed for very long because of the irony that God allowed me to see in the situation. I pray that when I leave the impact that I have made won't be as empty as that package of hot chocolate. I settled back and enjoyed the letter I had received that day from my youngest daughter, Kira.

My evening prayer: "Lord, please keep my heart in tune with Yours so that others will see You through me."

DAY #36   LEARNED OF DADDY'S DEATH

Tonight I learned of Daddy's death from Carl. This was the day of his funeral so there was no way I could go. I was playing Skip-Bo with Valerie, Holly, and Amber when I felt something pulling me to call Carl. It's hard to put my feelings on paper tonight so I'll reserve my thoughts for the morning.

DAY #37   THOUGHTS ON DADDY'S DEATH

It's 4:30 am on Wednesday, December seventeenth. I've been up since 3:30 with my usual routine. I wheel in the laundry cart with the "clean" towels and uniforms, washed and dried only hours earlier. I neatly go through seventy-five pairs of orange pants and shirts looking for the five sets I gather for four friends and myself. After I go through the towels looking for those I know, I separate the small dingy state towels from the white, fluffier and larger towels that were sent by loved ones on the outside. My chores of love continue as I sweep and mop the concrete floor around a six-bunk area where I sleep.

Mornings are my best time to collect my thoughts for paper. I can look out over a sea of gray state-issued blankets with an occasional white ripple of a personal blanket and all is calm and serene. As the others start to wake up and move around, I retreat to the privacy of my own bunk. This morning everything is still the same as I fix my coffee, light my cigarette and sit on the "front porch" (the small blank area at the front of the dorm) to do my thinking and my writing.

NO, everything is not the same, only the routine. The thought process keeps repeating the events of yesterday. It is hard to fathom how one could go from great joy to ultimate sorrow.

Maybe my getting sick after breakfast yesterday morning was just to set the tone for the day. My heart jumped when my name was called at mail call. I'd been worried and anxious that I would receive a letter from Mother in answer to the harsh but true statements I had sent her in regards to what she, my brother and Ms. X had taken from me.

41

Even though I had tried to convince myself that she no longer was a part of my life, the child within me was in fear of the scolding I would receive, deserved or not.

As I took the letter and noticed that it was from Catherine I could feel how heavy it was and I knew that she had finally sent my pictures. The envelope had already been opened and inspected for contraband so it wasn't hard to retrieve the photos I had waited so long to get.

In the stack was my grandson, with his crystal blue eyes and devilish grin, the sweet innocent face of my adorable Kira, my beautiful but tired-looking Catherine and several other various snapshots.

I proudly sought out those whom I had told about my kids and reveled in their "oohs" and "aahs" and how beautiful they all were. This was the happiest moment I've felt since I had been here. I didn't realize that my day would end with my lowest point in thirty days of incarceration or actually my life.

Catherine's letter mentioned that she had a court date on December 16th. Thank God she had included her Dad's new phone number and her new address.

I finally reached Carl at 8:30 or 9:00 pm. I could tell by his voice that something was wrong. As he started the old phrase, "I don't know how. . ." I interrupted him. "Daddy's dead, isn't he?" The phone was silent for a moment. I broke the tension by asking when he died. Carl said Friday but he didn't learn about it until Monday when he saw it in the paper. He said that he had called Catherine and she hadn't heard about it at all.

The funeral was yesterday and no one bothered to call me. Because I did not have any of their new addresses or phone numbers, I had been totally out of touch since Thursday.

The Lord does know what He's doing. After I found out what transpired at the funeral, it is probably a good thing that I wasn't there. My brother had the audacity to bar Catherine from the cemetery. He bluntly told her that she had brought enough shame to the family by bringing a "bastard" child into it. My sister-in-law was bold enough to stop Kira from going to her own grandmother. Apparently mother sat by and allowed all of this to happen.

I tried for the rest of the evening to reach Catherine at the phone number Carl gave me but she wasn't there. I wanted to be able to reach out and hug both she and Kira and apologize for the wrong done to them by my own flesh and blood.

Bobby now had what he always wanted, to be an only child, but I wonder if he is going to be able to accept the cost.

Needless to say, I had a hard time falling to sleep last night. Intermittent moments of praying and crying, not for the loss of my father because I knew where he was, but for the intense hurt my children must be feeling and for the first time I wasn't there to console them.

DAY #40   JAILHOUSE POSSESSIONS

It has been a little over a month since I arrived. I have finally come to terms that my world has been reduced to a metal bunk, 36" by 72", with a drawer 24"wide by 36" long by 9" deep. This space will now hold my "worldly possessions" for the time it is allotted for me to stay, however long God says that is.

At the best of times my possessions include a mattress that is comically referred to as a band aid, a pair of sheets, a personal double blanket, left to me by a departing inmate, and an illegal gray wool state blanket. It was only illegal because we were allowed either two personal blankets or one state blanket. All of this had to be kept on top of the bed, along with two personal towels, left to me by a friend. One of these towels I would use for my nightly shower and the other I used to wrap around a package of state supplied sanitary napkins, so that I would have a pillow. Real pillows are not allowed. I guess the reasoning behind this was to prevent one inmate from smothering another, as if a blanket couldn't be used. Under my mattress I usually kept my "rolling board" for cigarettes, my "writing board" or home-made cardboard desk with my current work-in-progress and whenever I left the dorm that is where I would stash the current book I was reading.

The small space at the foot of my bed not covered by mattress was used as an end table. I used it for my Bible, my makeshift ashtray and my insulated plastic coffee mug. All of this had to go into the drawer when we left the dorm, depending on which shift supervisor was on duty, or if we were told the "fire marshal" was on the compound.

Inside my drawer I had to accommodate my shampoo, two rolls of toilet paper, my comb, my pencils, pens and spoon, toothpaste, toothbrush, denture cream, Fed-ex envelopes used as folders to hold letters, papers and pictures, cigarettes, soap, any extra library books, my laundry bag, underwear, one pair of sweats, t-shirts and any other clothing I might acquire from departing inmates. Since we were not supposed to have anything under our mattress, my large flannel sleep shirt had to make its home between my sheets during the day. My drawer also had to hold any goodies that I was able to order from commissary.

Drawers are guarded as if they held the kings ransom. If you are fortunate to own a lock, you keep it locked at all times. If you are lulled into a feeling that you are only surrounded by friends, you are apt to loose a box of tobacco, a T-shirt or even a roll of toilet tissue. Toilet tissue is a very interesting subject in prison. It is one of your most prized possessions, especially when you are issued only two rolls a week. This precious commodity is not just used for the obvious reason but also for nose blowing, glass cleaning, wiping up spills and a variety of other uses. You guard it with your life. There is a legend in jail; if you were to leave a hundred dollar bill and a roll of toilet paper on your bunk and walked away, the hundred dollar bill would be there when you got back but the toilet paper wouldn't.

A false sense of security is very dangerous in jail when it comes to your priceless possessions. That is because of one important factor to remember; you are in jail. There are people in the same room with you because they are thieves. The saddest part of this is that most of those that will take your items are so use to doing it for survival on the outside that they have developed a diminished sense of right and wrong.

Another time that this is painfully obvious is when laundry comes back. Everyone rushes to the cart as soon as it is rolled in the door to gather their T-shirts, sweats, sleepwear, etc. Unfortunately, there are those who gather more than their own. Then accusations fly and the threat from the guards for a "shakedown" becomes imminent. Then, just as miraculously as the articles of clothing disappear, they suddenly reappear.

We all have something that could be considered contraband in our drawer or our bed. Whether it is two blankets, more than two towels, a pair of tweezers, or "love letters" from a fellow inmate. Even if you are one of the few who may be completely clean, you don't want to bring a shakedown on the comrades you have to live with.

DAY #41   HUMILIATION AS A DETERRENT

In the free world we express our sense of self by the clothing that we wear, the music that we enjoy, the furniture that we buy, the games that we play and what lifestyle we develop. When we are stripped of these material possessions we are also stripped of an integral part of one's self. This brings on a profound humiliation, along with knowing that we are able-bodied but lack the authority to do the simplest things for ourselves.

At chow time we must line up in our hall. We must wear institution issued clothing, and we must walk in a single file line along the gray tile blocks with our hands clasped behind our backs. We must sit where we are told, eat what is provided in the time allotted and return to our dorm only when we are told we may.

Prison will destroy you mentally, if you let it. Being in prison can be one of the most degrading experiences of your life. Prison is not about walls but more about mental breakdown. It becomes a war of wills and of minds.

Prison is a metaphor for failure, the failure of those who end up here, while a sense of self-worth is a foundation for active learning, for being willing to take risks.

I'm beginning to see that one of the greatest injustices in prison is also the surest form of control – humiliation by stripping our self-worth. Unfortunately this opens the door for some to find their own source of dignity and pride by preying upon the weak by building themselves up, while putting someone else down verbally or physically.

I'm learning very quickly that those predators usually are the ones whose hearts were their first victim.

DAY #45   CHRISTMAS LETTER TO MAMA

Merry Christmas! Once again I'll use a letter I wrote Mama as a way to express my feeling for this day, Christmas 2003.

Dear Mama,

As you might guess, Christmas is not a very festive time in jail. To most it's just another holiday they have to spend away from their children and other family members. Any remembrance of the season only brings sadness with thoughts of home.

The guards have tried to make things as pleasant as possible. There is the traditional tree in the hall with fake presents underneath. But, you can almost hear the sighs and moans of sadness each time we march pass it on the way to chow. Christmas Day will bring the traditional turkey and dressing dinner but there will be no blessing, except each one's private prayer, and no reading of the Christmas story as we did when I was a child. As hard as the guards try to bring Christmas cheer, the best that can be said it will be just another meal with a little more food.

For several days, different church groups have brought their Christmas cheer, with special services and treats of different varieties. It is amusing to see that some of these ladies who never go to church make a special point to attend these services for what they might receive, not necessarily spiritual. One group brought Christmas cookies and candies while another group handed out paper and pens in a nice little burlap pouch. Then one group of ladies actually came around to each dorm and gave every one of us our own paper sack with a cookie, a crocheted cross bookmark, a package of sugar and a package of cream, a peppermint candy cane and a couple of pecans.

While these things might seem simple to you, we held each item in deep regard. I still have the cross book mark and will hold on to it forever, for it is not only a reminder of the love that Christ had for me but the love that true Christians are capable of showing when they follow Christ's instructions in Matthew 25:40. "Inasmuch as ye have done it unto the least of these my brethren, ye have done it unto Me."

This is the night before Christmas Eve and the dorm is the normal beehive of activity. Nothing more or less than usual. Some are getting their hair fixed or braided; card games are being played in almost every corner of the dorm; some, like me, are writing letters while others are just visiting.

In the front corner of the room surprisingly there is a Christmas special playing on the television and a couple of the ladies are actually watching, but most everyone else is ignoring it as they try and ignore that Christmas is only a "wake-up" away.

One thing I have noticed is Christmas specials are usually avoided as much as possible, especially those that could possibly have someone singing "I'll Be Home For Christmas." This particular special must have slipped through because it featured religious songs of Christmas. Those are a little easier to handle because they allow you to focus more on the "the Reason for the Season" instead of your own misery and homesickness.

Everyone seemed impervious to the carol that was being sung over the TV. That is until I took a closer look. One by one, I started to notice the faint movement of lips discretely mouthing the words along with the singer, without missing a beat of their current activity. "Silent night, Holy Night. All is calm, all is bright."

Christmas is here, alive and well, but for most of us self-preservation won't allow the bubbling enthusiasm we'd show if we were in the free world. Actually in a way it has allowed me to experience a Christmas without all the commercialism, the scurrying around and the frustration that the Christmas season usually brings.

With my current accommodations, my thought, more than ever before, turn to what the first Christmas must have been like as Mary gave birth to our Lord and King.

I am so blessed that the Lord has given me this opportunity to be able to cut everything else out of my life and concentrate just on Him this Christmas.

One of the things that I am wondering as I lay here on the eve of our Lord's birth is where were your thoughts this holiday season?

Love always,
Your daughter, Tracey

DAY #51   MY FRIEND VALERIE

Daily Blessing - *Proverbs 18:24. "A man that hath friends must show himself friendly: and there is a friend that sticketh closer than a brother."*

Most people don't believe you can make lasting friendships in jail. In fact, the advice given to inmates is, "don't trust anyone," or, "don't talk to anyone." I admit to you that there are valid reasons for this at times, but I've got a marvelous exception to this rule.

God puts certain people in our lives to meet a special need, or for you to meet a special need for them Then you move off in different directions. There are others that remain friends throughout life. God sends friends who share your disappointments, your hopes, your highs and your lows. They see your faults and love you anyway. You learn to resolve conflict, trust one another. God sent such a friend to me in Valerie.

I remember the first time I met her. I had been in a lockdown cell for several days before any beds became available in C Dorm. I mentioned to an inmate, who also attributed her incarceration to the notorious Ms. X, that I had to get out of lockdown because it was driving me crazy. Several minutes later I was called to the door to move my mattress and few possessions to bed #74 in C Dorm. Valerie was directly behind me in bed #75, at the very back of the dorm.

I had noticed her only in passing when I was in the dorm during the day. Directly across from Valerie was Robin. Robin had gotten some bad drugs along the way and partially "fried her brain," but she was a sweet girl; strange but sweet.

Valerie rolled cigarettes for cookies and tootsie pops since she no longer smoked. On Thursday, my first day to witness the madness of commissary, Robin told Valerie to give me half of the box of the tobacco she was rolling.

Valerie was very stoic and stern looking. To be honest, I was a little scared of her at first. I later learned that she was a very sensitive and caring individual whom others turned to for advice.

Valerie was no saint. Even though she didn't really look like she belonged in a place like this and her intelligence level was far greater than most, I learned about her checkered past over the next ensuing weeks and months.

Valerie was in for selling "dope" to an undercover agent in Bossier, but it wasn't her first experience with incarceration. Drugs and all that drugs bring into one's life had been a major part of her life.

Because of the beds being in the back of the dorm and farthest away from the guard's window, we were able to have late night chats after lights out. I began to look forward to our evening chats. I also watched Valerie as she counseled some of the girls with their legal and emotional problems

Valerie was my mentor. She taught me so many things. Things I would need to know to survive in that place. She passed along her culinary skills of making burritos and brownies, her dexterity skills in rolling cigarettes, so that I would get more than the usual 36 cigarettes from a box. She also taught me the emotional skills of toughening myself as much as possible.

On New Years' Eve I was making cards to go with the bracelets that I had Doris make for Valerie, Holly, Amber and myself to commemorate our friendship into the new year. In trying to write one poem including all of their traits,

I kept writing verses that pertained mainly to Valerie and what her friendship meant to me.

FOR MY FRIEND, VALERIE

Whatever did I do
To deserve a friend like you?
What untold deed did I accomplish
To be rewarded with a friend so true?

How can I tell you what your friendship means?
Words just aren't ever enough.
You cared for me, protected me,
And taught me to be tough.

God brought us together,
This I'll never doubt.
Our friendship will continue
Whether we are in jail or out.

I hope, dear friend, we stay in touch
And never lose one another.
For such a treasured friend like you
Could never be replaced by any other.

Our time together is fleeting
And one day we must part.
No matter what the future holds.
You'll always have a place in my heart.

One day the gates will open
And we both will be gone.
To continue down life's highway
With a prayer our friendship will go on.

But if our pathways never cross
And your face I never see.
When Christ comes in all His glory
I'm sure in Heaven we both will be.

DAY #52   NEW YEAR'S DAY

Daily Blessing - *Revelations 21:5 And He that sat upon the throne said, Behold, I make all things new. And He said unto me, Write: for these words are true and faithful."*

Happy New Year! I have experienced a lot of New Years in my life, but this one will probably stand out in my mind more than any other. After we had our black-eyed peas and cabbage for lunch, the guards decided that the kitchen staff needed the night off, so we had sack lunches for supper.

When it was time to roll for chow, we were instructed to sit on our beds as sack lunches were passed out to each of us. The meal consisted of a tuna-fish sandwich, a bag of chips and a cookie. Three friends joined me as we had a "picnic on the grounds," even though "the grounds" was a concrete floor.

We discussed with other inmates where we might be and what we might be doing if we were at home. Most of them had to admit that they would probably be stoned or drunk "out of their mind." As sad as it sounds, several even admitted that if God and the law hadn't intervened, they would probably be dead.

I even had a couple of the girls confess that this was the first "sober" New Year's that they had experienced in many, many years. That night instead of turning to drugs or booze for a momentary thrill, many of us turned to praising God for a permanent high that would never go away.

God showed me through all of this that sometimes before we can start something new we have to end some old things, first.

My New Year's resolution for this year is more in the form of a prayer:

MY NEW YEAR'S RESOLUTION

Lord, a new year is beginning
And I'm turning my resolutions over to You.
Help me be more Christ like
In everything I say and do.

Help me to be more forgiving
Of those that mean me only harm.
Let me feel safe and secure
As I lean upon Your protective arm.

As I face the trials and tribulations of this year
Help me keep my faith and heart on You.
Don't every let me forget whatever comes
There's nothing the two of us can't do.

For the final part of my resolution
That I am turning over to You today
Keep me aware You're always with me
Whatever may come my way.

DAY #66   TWENTY-THIRD PSALM

Daily Blessing – Psalm 23

As I lay in my bunk tonight I reread the 23rd Psalm and the Lord helped me understand it in a whole different manner.

THE LORD IS MY SHEPHERD – A shepherd's job is to tend his flock. Whether it is protection from the elements, wolves or any other danger that his charge might fall prey. He is ever present, on guard every moment. Just as God's omnipresence and supreme protection surrounds me.

I SHALL NOT WANT – It doesn't say, I shall not need, it says "I shall not want." As a loving Father, God not only supplies my needs but also my wants as long as they and I are in the center of His will and one in mind and spirit with Him.

HE MAKETH ME TO LIE DOWN IN GREEN PASTURES – Sometimes God makes me stop and smell the roses. Too many times I am so busy striving for something bigger that I don't take the time to see the wonderful gifts that God has provided me, free of charge.

HE LEADS ME BESIDE STILL WATERS – How many times do I call for God's guidance when the waters of life are rough and choppy? How many times should I call on His leadership during the "still waters" when I think I can control it on my own?

HE RESTORES MY SOUL – All too often the pressure and struggle of everyday life drains my very being down to my soul. Especially when I try to tackle life on my own, but God is always there to restore me and refresh me with His love and forgiveness.

HE LEADS ME IN THE PATHS OF RIGHTOUSNESS FOR HIS NAME SAKE – One of the most precious gifts a father gives his child is his name. I was raised to respect that name, to avoid bringing shame upon it because it is a reflection upon him. How different is it with me and the name my Heavenly Father has given me, "Christian"? If I let Him, He will "lead me in the paths of righteousness" so I don't bring shame and retribution to it.

YEA, THOUGH I WALK THROUGH THE VALLEY OF THE SHADOW OF DEATH I WILL FEAR NO EVIL; FOR THOU ART WITH ME – Yes, God's protection is available to me when I stumble into areas that present a danger to me but this verse says "walk through," not run, not stumble but deliberately walk, with eyes wide open. Whether this means the drug addict trying for that ultimate high that will put them in the "valley of the shadow of death" or the alcoholic getting behind the wheel of a car that endangers not only their lives but all those around them. God will be there, if they only ask. He will take them by the hand and lead them through it. At the same time He will lead them without fear away from the evil that is destroying their lives.

YOUR ROD AND YOUR STAFF, THEY COMFORT ME – A shepherd uses his rod and his staff for protection of his sheep and for chastisement. When I was a child, I feared my father's punishment but I also had a certain amount of comfort in knowing his punishment for my wrongdoing was a sign of his love for me. How can it be any different with my Heavenly Father?

YOU PREPARE A TABLE BEFORE ME IN THE PRESENCE OF MINE ENEMIES – One of the times that I am most vulnerable is when I am eating. How wonderful and reassuring it is that God can give me the peace that passes all understanding to be able to sit down and enjoy a feast with my enemies (physical or spiritual) lurking in the shadows?

YOU ANNOINT MY HEAD WITH OIL, MY CUP RUNNETH OVER – When God gives me His anointing, it doesn't diminish what He has to give but multiplies it beyond measure, to the point of overflowing. This is true for all of the Gifts of God from His unending love to my humanly wants and needs.

SURELY GOODNESS AND MERCY SHALL FOLLOW ME ALL THE DAYS OF MY LIFE – The Bible commonly refers to God as a "just" God, but thank goodness for my sake He is also a merciful God. If I have to choose between justice and mercy, give me mercy every time. That's what God does. He first showed me mercy by sending His only "natural" Son to die for the sins of His "adopted" child. How much more merciful can you get?

AND I WILL DWELL IN THE HOUSE OF THE LORD FOREVER – With all these wonderful affirmations of God's love, His protection, His promises and His salvation would it not be stupid of me to not take Him at His promise of my "adoption" into His family through my faith in Jesus Christ? Because of my acceptance of God as my Heavenly Father, I have all the rights, duties and privileges that come with family membership.

DAY #68   SHAKY

Daily Blessing – *Hebrews 13:2.* *"We should not forget to entertain strangers, lest we entertain angels unaware"*

We are all angels or have the possibility of being an angel to someone else. This became very obvious to me through a lovely lady named, Keri.

Several days before Christmas, we got a particularly interesting inmate. I didn't notice her when she first came in, but as I glanced around the room I saw what appeared to be a blanket waded up by the front door. Upon closer examination, I found there to be a small, older female tightly encased within; wet and shivering.

This had not been the first prisoner brought in with DT's (withdrawals) so I assumed this to be the case with "Shaky." This was a nickname we later gave her. Every one of us seems to have a nickname but I'll cover that later.

As the self-appointed welcoming committee, I offered her a cup of hot coffee and an ear. She didn't hesitate in accepting my offer and told me the story of how she had just moved to Monroe to care for her mother in the later stages of Alzheimer's. This is something I really could relate to, having watched my own father suffer with his diseases for several years.

There was a neighbor across the street from her that suffered the same affliction and Shaky kept a close eye on her. Somehow the neighbor mistook Shaky good intentions as troublesome and called the police to report Shaky making harassing phone calls. The police came to arrest Shaky, but she had taken her nightly sleeping pill and was uncooperative. She was placed in a cold shower. Even though Shaky was small in stature, she fought back against the officers and the water. In the scuffle she managed to break a couple of ribs.

The officers took her to the hospital before bringing her to RPDC but she was made to sit in a cold drafty hall for several hours before the attending physician could see her. She was shaking from the cold, not from any withdrawal symptoms.

Shaky knew no one in the area so she had no one to call to help her out. Several of us managed to get in touch with the unofficial chaplain, Brother Bradley. He helped her to not only get out but to get the charges dropped against her.

She promised before she left that she would write and also send some things for those that couldn't afford some of their necessary items. She was so grateful for all we had done to help her that she said that she felt that she had to do something in return. Over the last few months I had heard several promises like that which never came to fruition.

But, I saw that Shaky did keep her promise to write. I got a letter from her today. It's comforting to know that her life has returned to normal, or as normal as anyone's life could be after experiencing this place.

She wanted a copy of the package list and wanted to know if I would accept the items and disperse them to those that needed them the most.

My evening prayer: "Thank You, Lord, for letting me see that in helping others I open myself to your blessings. And, thank you, Father, for not only sending your angels but the entertaining forms You use."

DAY #69   EXPENDABILITY

It has been over two months since this nightmare began. Maybe nightmare isn't the correct terminology. There have been good moments, learning moments, but on the whole, the greatest factor to overcome has been the loss of control; loss of control on what is going on with the outside world. Constant thoughts of, "If I were out I could get this taken care of," or, "If I were out I could salvage that." But the stark realization is that you are not out and the only link between you and the free world is a telephone line which is quite expensive, or a letter that takes three or four days to arrive at its destination.

Besides the loss of control there is the hidden emotion that you are expendable; that life and the world goes on without you. As a mother, it is an extremely hard reality to face that your kids can survive without you. Yes, you've raised them to be self-sufficient and independent, but you always expected to be in the wings waiting to catch them if they fell.

Now they are not only having to pick themselves up, but also they to brush themselves off and continue on. The sense of pride that you have succeeded in your mission as a mother is momentarily overshadowed by the fact that maybe you succeeded too well.

Will things be any different when you get out and resume life in the free world? How can it? Your life and those around you will always be marked by this forced separation.

Sundays are always a bad day for me to write because it is visitation day and I know my name won't be called Yet, I listen as each name is called, hoping beyond hope that they made that extra effort, especially this Sunday with my birthday only a few days away.

Once again, the loss of control takes over. I don't know if it's lack of transportation, or if the baby is sick. Is it lack of money or just lack of interest? *When you have too much time to think, all kinds of scenarios pass through your head.*

The only way to find peace is to put it in God's hands and ask that He watch over your precious children until you can once again be reunited with them.

DAY #70   JAILHOUSE FRIENDSHIP

What I feel will be the saddest part of my time here came today. I was taking my usual morning nap when the whole bed shook. Valerie had slammed her drawer right at my head. I came straight up to see why she was so mad. The first thing that caught my eye was the white plastic tub; the one that the guards bring in on DOC moving day. Valerie was now "DOC" and had to be transferred.

I felt as though someone had ripped out my heart. I wished I had been given more time to tell her just how I felt about her, how appreciative I was for all she'd done for me and how much I loved her for it.

I don't know how I would have made it through without her. One of the major things that she taught me was something she never knew. After what I'd just been through with family and friends I had lost all hope of ever trusting anyone again. Valerie taught me there were people in this world, like her, that I could trust.

One afternoon after mail call I found Valerie sitting on her bed weeping over a card she was holding. She had received a letter from her father telling her that he was behind her and loved her.

In talking to her I could hear in her voice the regret that she had over the life that she had chosen and how it had affected all of those around her. This next poem was the best way I could express it for her and all of the others that come to this realization.

THE YOU, YOU SHOULD HAVE BEEN

You feel the pain of those you've hurt
This time it's even more.
Their pain isn't any different
From all the times before.

But now you've come to realize
Why their hurt is deep within.
It's only 'cause they can see
The you, you should have been.

Now you know the reason
For all their grief and sorrow.
You can start to make the change
That will bring all a better tomorrow.

The punishment you've been given
Is not yours alone.
It's felt by all that love you
Especially those at home.

Nothing can erase the scars
Caused by what you've done.
But faith in God can heal the hurt
Through Jesus Christ, His Son.

And those you love will soon be comforted
And feel a peace within.
Knowing you and God are on the path
To the you, you should have been.

The day she went to court for her sentencing I wrote the
following poem to let her know I was praying for her. I'm

glad she has it with her to remind her that I always will have her in my thoughts and prayers, no matter where we might be.

I STOPPED AND SAID A PRAYER FOR YOU

I stopped and said a prayer for you
'Cause you were on my mind.
I prayed all your trouble, cares and woes
Would soon be far behind.

I prayed that God would give you strength
For all the tough times ahead.
I prayed for the peace that only He can give
When you put yourself to bed.

I prayed that you'd be surrounded
With friends as wonderful as you.
To help you past the rough times
And be there to see you through.

I stopped and said a prayer for you
And will forever more.
That God will pour out His blessings on you
And amaze you with all He has in store.

So, as you go from day to day.
And you feel a warm tug at your heart.
You'll know I stopped and said a prayer for you
Whether we're near or far apart.

There was a time before she was snatched from me that things got rocky between us, but I think the Lord was preparing me for the time that would be inevitable, a time I would have to stand alone.

Thank you, my dear friend, for making me a better person and a better prisoner so I can help the new ones coming in. I hope I can be at least half the example to them that you were to me.

DAY #71   AMBER GOES HOME

Tomorrow I will lose another friend to the free world. Amber will be going home. Whether the inmate is disliked by all or she is the favorite one in the dorm, her departure brings the same response of clapping and cheering from everyone. It's like there is a glimmer of hope that soon you, too, will be walking out of those doors.

There is always a feeling of joy for them but a little jealously that it's not you and sometimes the nagging question: "Will they be back?" You knew that some will be, if not here, another jail, somewhere.

DAY #72   SOUNDS IN JAIL

As my "holding" time wears on, I find myself trying to sleep it away. Whether it is escape from the reality around me or just sheer boredom, I find ways to nap as often as possible. But even in dreamland there are several sounds that my ears have become attuned to

The first is, "Line up for chow." This call comes three times a day and is the one sure escape from the 54 foot by 108 foot room where I spend most of my time.

The second greatest sound is, "Mail Call." This is the time of day that you can actually link to the world outside. After mail call comes the listing of names of those that have packages. These are usually a mixture of essentials from deodorant, shampoo, towels, blankets, etc. These are things we take for granted on the outside but mean a little touch of home while we are here. There are certain times of the year that you can get packages, and then the contents can only be what the higher ups deem necessary.

Once a week, on Thursday morning, you sit anxiously after breakfast, waiting for your name to be called to pick up your "commissary." Your weekly supply of cigarettes, Pepsi's, coffee and whatever treats you can afford from the monies sent by those on the outside.

Several times a week some listen for "Church" to be called. This is another opportunity to get out of the dorm, if only for an hour.

On rare occasions you are allowed to venture outside for fifteen to thirty minutes into a 60-foot by 100-foot pen of chain link and razor wire, with barbed wire thrown in for good measure.

There is one other rare and beautiful sound. As Simon and Garfunkel labeled it, "The Sound of Silence." This is the sound when everyone has finally settled down for the night and all of the talking and giggling has ceased. 75 ladies are either sleeping, reading, or writing letters.

After all of the hollering, chattering and other noises of the day, this is the most welcomed sound.

DAY #73   55TH BIRTHDAY

Daily Blessing – *Isaiah 44:24 "Thus saith the LORD, thy Redeemer, and He that formed thee from the womb, I am the LORD that maketh all things; that stretcheth forth the heavens alone; that spreadeth abroad the earth by Myself"*

Happy Birthday to me! It is my birthday, my 55ᵗʰ birthday.

I think the best way to describe my birthday is to quote from the letter I wrote Mama a few minutes ago.

> *"This birthday was one of the best I have ever had. These ladies made sure of that. Several gave up a package of cookies and a candy bar from commissary to make me three birthday brownies. Another friend gave up a whole box of cigarette to pay a girl to make me a handmade cross necklace, woven from purple and white trash bags, but it was more precious and beautiful than the finest diamond cross in any store. Another spent a half a bag of coffee for a poem where each verse typified a particular quality they saw in me. Each of these verses and qualities spelled out my name, "Tracey". The whole day was spent with birthday congratulations from those that had become close, and by those that just knew me as "Nana."*
>
> *So you see, God knew what He was doing. This birthday, more than ever, I've learned the people I can count on and those I can't. I've also found a greater appreciation for the two beautiful daughters I have and the wonderful grandson God's given me."*

This afternoon my name was called for a package. Shaky had come through with what she had promised. She didn't know it was my birthday, but God did. It couldn't have been arranged any better.

I stood in extreme anticipation as I waited for my box to be inspected. I watched as the bottles of lotion, bars of soap, shampoos, towel, flannel sheets, and an assortment of games were lifted from the box, inspected and approved.

When I got the box back to the dorm, the vultures soon descended on me before I could get through the door. I shared most of what was in the box, except for the flannel sheets, the chess game, two decks of cards, and an extra large, heavy pink flannel nightshirt with a fuzzy kitten on the front.

The most prized possession that I received from my angel was something quite a few couldn't understand; four tubes of denture cream. Until you have dentures and have nothing to hold them in, you can't truly appreciate the ability to eat. Once again, all the simple luxuries you have a tendency to forget about until they become a valued necessity.

My evening prayer: "Once again, Father, I must thank you for all the angels in my life and how much joy and understanding you have brought me through them. Let me be ever mindful that I, too, need to be an angel in others lives so they can see Your love. Also, Father, tonight I humbly thank you giving me another year and another chance to fully appreciate You and all Your magnificence."

DAY #74   MANDY ARRIVES

My children and their friends have always seemed to gravitate toward me and my home. This is not a bad thing. At least I always knew where they were. Today, I was reminded of this even more than ever. Mandy, my unofficial daughter, showed up here at Rayville as an inmate, not a visitor.

I had been a part of Mandy's life since she was 14. She was my oldest daughter's half sister and she had gone through a messy divorce between her father (my ex-husband) and her mother. During a period of time that she lived with me, she adopted me as her, "Mama." She told us that she felt more love at our house than she felt anywhere else.

I know now that I can say without any provocation that I can't even go to jail and get away from my kids.

Mandy isn't what you'd really label as a bad kid, just misdirected. For two years her father and mother fought over her custody. Her father wanted what was best for her and her mother, for not wanting her father to have her. For two whole years, Mandy was the center of attention and then the divorce was granted. Her father got custody and all the fuss and mayhem was over.

Mandy then decided to make her own. There were incidences of stealing her father's truck while he was seriously ill in the hospital, and wrecking it, to minor mischief around the trailer park. Mandy then hit the "big time" and stole her own mother's truck while her mother was at work. Her mother pressed charges and Mandy wound up here.

I can't be real sure if it was to punish Mandy or me. I'm sure the Lord will get us through this one.

My evening prayer: "Lord, I come to you tonight asking for your Divine Guidance in working with Mandy. Please, Lord, show me the way to reach her heart and her mind so she can keep them more in tune with You. Lord, please help me be the example she needs. Father, please help me to show her that life behind bars is a poor substitution for the love she so desperately seeks. Help me show her that love can be found only in You."

* One month later, Mandy's mom dropped the charges she had in Bossier Parish for unauthorized use of a vehicle, but Mandy wasn't allowed to go straight home. She had taken her mother's keys in Caddo parish and she faced felony charges for that incident. She was transferred to Caddo Parish until the release could be worked out there. Unfortunately she didn't abide by the provisions of her probation on some other charges she faced in Bossier and was returned to Bossier Sheriff's Correction Facility for probation violation, several months after I was released from RPDC. She has until April, 2007, this time, to learn a lesson she didn't seem to learn the first time around. God be with her, I pray.

DAY #80   SAMANTHA

Daily Blessing – Romans 8:28 *"And we know that all things work together for good to them that love God, to them who are the called according to His purpose."*

My mind has been racing for days trying to get my facts together about my case. Who heard Ms. X tell me to use the credit card? Who heard her tell how we ordered computers so we could teach computer classes? I was sitting outside when one of the girls who had gone to Benton for sentencing the previous day, came running to me and told me that she had a surprise for me. She said they had brought back three other females from Benton and wanted me to meet them. That's when she introduced me to Samantha, Beth, and Leslie.

As we talked I noticed that Samantha kept looking at me with a quizzical look on her face. Finally she blurted out, "You're Tracey Brown! You're the one my son keeps talking about." That's when I found out that Samantha was the mother to one of the painter's union officials that Ms. X had bragged to about the computers and how we would work out a special deal with all the members to learn computers. I now had his name, address and phone number and his mother's assurance that he would do anything possible to help me because he knew the whole story.

It doesn't take many incidences that like to soon see the Lord does answer prayers: sometimes in more direct ways than others.

* *Much later on, Samantha had a heart attack and they sent her St. Gabriel for medical reasons. We later learned she had another heart attack while there and died.*

DAY #81   TIFFANY

Shortly before Valerie left, I was blessed with a new bunkmate directly in front of me, Tiffany. Tiffany was an attractive woman in her forties. She had a certain look of class that didn't quite seem to belong here. I never really asked what brought her to jail but she eventually told me the story over a period of time.

She had been dating a certain young man whose truck she borrowed one night, without his permission. He pressed charges of "unauthorized use of a moveable" which is a misdemeanor as opposed to "felony auto theft."

Tiffany was one of the many whose "occasional" partying with cocaine, particularly crack, became an overwhelming everyday obsession. Tiffany was an intelligent woman who had commanded salaries of seventy-thousand plus a year. She not only smoked it all up, but also went a step further and "borrowed" over eight thousand dollars from her employer.

She later learned from her sister that her former employer was pending charges of fraud and embezzlement, but only after she finished the time required for her parole violation (her boyfriend had her pawn a gun in her name) and the misdemeanor charge outstanding. These charges she will face in Caddo, not Bossier.

She, like several of us, was now homeless, without any worldly possessions and penniless. This was such a waste of a beautiful young life. Several of the inmates had relayed stories of their history of drug use. It was as if they were talking about a lover.

Tiffany made a statement that caused me to stop and think and eventually gave me the idea for this poem. She said, *"Drugs are a very jealous lover. I am speaking from so much personal experience, here. An addict can not love themselves or anyone else when they are using. The drug is our lover, our mistress, our significant other. There is no room for anybody else, no matter how bad they want it. The drug is our Higher Power. It's as simple as that. All I did, I did for my drug"*

Another interesting point to this poem was the reaction it caused when others read it. The original title I chose, "For Tiffany," because her experience had been the focal point of my inspiration.

As others started reading I could see the puzzled looks on their faces as they wondered just where this poem was going. I could tell when they got about halfway through; their faces lit up like a light bulb in understanding. Some of the more experienced drug users didn't take that long to figure it out.

LOVE AFFAIR

When we first met,
Fast friends we became.
How were you to know
It was all just a game?

I let you learn to like me
Then likeness turned to love.
I had you in my power
Without a single shove.

I won you over quickly,
Like all of those before.
You didn't even realize
When you stepped through the door.

The times we spent together
Were only to be brief.
But you craved me more and more.
There was to be no relief.

Our flirtation turned to obsession,
Then I took the upper hand.
By then you were too weak
To even make a stand.

By then all you had
Was soon to be mine.
I knew it from the start.
It was just a matter of time.

First, I took your wealth.
On me you spent every dime.
After all your money was gone,
You turned to a life of crime.

Your family was the next to go
Along with your car and home.
Leaving you all alone
With just the streets to roam.

Your health and mine are waning
Because of your abuse of me.
And your end will soon be coming,
This I can plainly see.

I've ruined your life,
I've destroyed your soul
To even remember your name
On your mind puts a toll.

When you are gone,
As soon you will be,
Who will I turn to?
Someone you turned on to me.

See, I'm not a person.
I've become a part of your life.
I go by many names
But in the end, it's always strife.
Some call me pot, cocaine
Or crack or dope.
No matter what you call me
I take away all hope.

So, next time you shoot up,
Hit that pipe or joint
You've done nothing more
Than help me prove my point.

I am a selfish lover
Who wants all of you.
And I won't release my hold
Until your time is through.

It's now your decision
Which lover you must choose.
My only guarantee is this
"With me you'll only lose."

Wouldn't this world be an amazing place if we each could feel this kind of passion for Christ!

Tracey Brown

* On March 15 Tiffany was moved to A Dorm. I began to see the pattern of people being moved in and out of my life for two purposes, what I could learn from them and what I could pass on to others about them. After much consideration I figured it was time to rename the poem, "The Love Affair" because it fit so many others I have come to know.

DAY #82   BUILDING WALLS FOR HEART SURVIVAL

Daily Blessing – *Psalm 4:8 "I will both lay me down in peace, and sleep: for Thou, LORD, only maketh me dwell in safety."*

When I first came to Rayville, I felt very strongly that the Lord had sent me as an observer. At first it was easy to stand back and report with a certain amount of objectivity, but the longer I am here, the closer I become to certain ones and my objectivity fails.

When you are confined for twenty-four hours a day, seven days a week; eating, sleeping, talking and all waiting for release day, you can't help getting close to some of those around you.

Then the stark realization hits you right between the eyes one day. Very soon you are going to have to say goodbye and probably never see some of those with whom you have formed a bond.

This realization has brought out a self-defense mechanism that I thought I had put away years ago; "the wall." If you build a wall around yourself and not allow yourself to become close to people, there will be no pain when you have to part. How reticent our body and heart is to avoiding pain and hurt.

Friendship in jail is a very fragile thing. Women by nature need a certain amount of camaraderie and affection (not just the passionate type.) They find this through friendship. When you first find yourself locked up with another 74 plus women, you can't help but gravitate toward those that you feel fit your needs closer than any of the others. Unfortunately with a pre-trial dorm people are very transient. What might have been a friendship that would have lasted a lifetime can be ripped apart by transfer to another dorm or going home. Out of the twenty or twenty-five that have left and promised to write, only two have done so.

After a few experiences of having my heart ripped apart, I started pulling away to a safe distance.

You also learn early on that some become friends because of the size of your commissary drawer or package contents. These are also the ones that become your "best bud" when they see you packing your stuff to leave. Each one of them wants something. They figure you are getting out and can replace it all. It's kind of like driving down the road and seeing a fresh road kill being picked apart by a bevy of vultures.

DAY #89   DADDY'S 86TH BIRTHDAY

It would have been Daddy's 86th birthday and, understandably, my thoughts turn to him, today. It's getting to the point where the Lord is allowing me to express some of my feelings more and more in poetic form.

IN MY DREAMS

I dreamed about you last night, Daddy
And some of the fun we had.
Like going to Uncle Austin's fishing camp
It was a lot of the good, none of the bad.

My dream made me realize,
Our good times together were all too few.
I'm not blaming you, Daddy
I know you had work to do.

Now that you are gone,
Your absence has caused my mind to wander.
Over times with my own children
How many good times are there for them to ponder?

Was I so absorbed in making a living
I didn't make time to make a life?
Was I always there to listen to them
About their achievements and their strife?

Or did I just shun them away,
The way you often did to me?
And let someone else hear their problems,
And let someone else share their glee.

I know now I should have done things differently.
I pray to God it's not too late to start.
I can't change things from the past,
Just start taking life a little more to heart.

So thank you, Dad, for all the good times
And for the lessons I learned from you.
For now, even in my dreams
I'm still learning the things I need to do.

DAY #100   DORIS'S STORY

One of the sweetest, dearest souls I met while here was a lady named Doris. She was in her forties and suffered from lupus. The effects of the disease had caused her face to become scarred, but once I got to know her, I easily could see past her scars into her heart through her crystal blue eyes.

Doris had six sons, one of whom was in prison in California, doing a life sentence for murder. Several of her other sons were in prisons around the country for various and sundry charges.

Doris had gotten into a scrap with her "old man", Bryan, and somehow a hot plate landed on the floor of the motel room and burned the carpet. When the police arrived, Doris was charged with aggravated battery with a hot plate.

Doris always loved my poetry and asked me to write a poem called, "House of Pain." That is all she gave me, just the title. The Lord took it from there and this poem was the result. It wasn't hard finding subject matter. All I had to do was what writers do best, sit back and look around the room and observe. Doris was thrilled with the end results and the fact that she inspired the poem.

HOUSE OF PAIN

A mother is in the corner
Racked with pain and tears,
Knowing her children are crying for her
Their hearts are full of doubts and fears.

Someone stands at the window
Thinking of the love she left behind.
Even though he beat and abused her
The good times are all that's on her mind.

The glassy stare of another
Trying to hide her pain within.
Regretting the life of drugging
That kept things from what might have been.

Another sits on her bed crying
Over the time she must spend
Trying to pay for the wrongs she's done
Wondering when it all will end.

Then there are those
That stole in one way or another.
The punishment is not theirs alone
For little babies are left without a mother.

They all share one thing in common
Whatever brought them to this place.
The hurt and shame is not theirs alone
It's something friends and loved ones must also face.

The stories all are different
But the hurt is all the same.
Each one must face their fears
In this constant "House of Pain."

* *On March 9, Doris rode into Benton with those of us who were scheduled for court. The van pulled up to the gas station across from the courthouse and let her out. She was going home. All charges had been dropped.*

DAY #106   HANDLING VIOLENCE

Daily Blessing – *II Timothy 1:7 "For God hath not given us the spirit of fear; but of power, and of love, and of a sound mind."*

Momentary flights of fancy in here make it extremely hard for true friendship to flourish. Every action, every word, every smile is judged by inmates and guards alike. So many times the jilted lover takes revenge through physical fights. The result is that "any" contact is a sign of brewing trouble.

Such an incident happened this morning while standing in line for lunch. One girl that had been linked with another decided their time was over and started flirting with another girl while standing in line. Before anyone knew it, a fight broke out that had to be handled by the guards.

You quickly learn whenever a fight ensues; just get out of the way. If you step in to stop it, you'll get hurt or thrown in lockdown for fighting.

So the survival of the heart becomes a prime responsibility if you expect to keep your sanity in here.

Since the old adage, "Your eyes are the windows to your soul," I guess the "game" we all must play is learning how to "tint" the windows so NO ONE can peek in at our vulnerability, whether it be guards or inmates, because like a crouching tiger, they will sense the weakness and jump on it in a heart beat.

DAY #111   SHARING

Sharing takes on a whole new meaning behind bars. Normally, "on the streets," you would offer a stranger a cookie from a package and not think a thing about it. In jail every morsel becomes worth its weight in gold. The favorite time for snacking is late at night when all of the lights go out. As you lay in your bed reading or writing you can hear paper rattling (there is no way to muffle the sound of cellophane) or the crunch, crunch of Cheetos, Fritos, or some other equally noisy treat.

This next poem was my first attempt at humor to commemorate the highest point of the week; Thursday morning when commissary is handed out. Orders that were placed on the previous Friday for cigarettes, coffee, Pepsi's and treats are neatly bagged and delivered, one by one as they call your name.

Hard as most of us try, very few (if any) have anything remaining on the night before commissary; therefore, this poem was born.

THE NIGHT BEFORE COMMISSARY

'Twas the night before commissary
And all through the dorm
People were bumming and begging
It had gotten to be the norm
With me in my night shirt
All ready for bed
My drawer was so empty
Not even a mouse could be fed.
Everyone was so hungry
For a noodle, cracker or pop.
But the drawers were all lacking

Not even a box of Top.
The lights all went off
It was peaceful and calm.
I laid in my bed
Reading from the book of Psalm.
When from the middle of the room
There rose such a clatter.
Paper rustling and rattling
What it was didn't matter.
I jumped from my bed
To find the source of the rattle.
I'd share if I must
But I'd sure never tattle.
I snuck by each bed
And listened under each cover.
'Til I heard the munching
And I started to hover.
I ripped off the blanket,
Tore off the sheet.
There was the evidence
A cookie wrapper right at her feet.
The crumbs on her face
Were a very good sign.
I was going to bed hungry
On that I must resign.
But I heard her exclaim
As I stomped out of sight,
"Save some of your goodies next week
And you won't have a famished night."

Earlier I mentioned a young girl named Beth that came
from Benton, with Samantha. Beth was in her late twenties,
about the same age of Catherine and in a lot of ways
reminded me of her. You could tell Beth had come from

money. Her family at one time owned a couple of jewelry stores. For some unknown reason she looked to me for guidance. Several times, when I wasn't able to make store, Beth ordered my cigarettes and wouldn't let me pay her back.

She was arrested with her boyfriend on a possession with intent to distribute charge. Her parents, who had been divorced, hired Daryl Gold as her attorney. He was able to get her bond reduced enough that they were able to get her out less than 30 days after she got here.

The night before she left she said I had not written a poem for her. After lights went out I slipped this to her bed. It was not only about her but all the young ones I had seen come and go.

Beth has written and sent several cards since she left. She also left me her sweat suit which I still cherish. I'll always be thankful for her.

WHAT ARE YOU DOING HERE?

What are you doing here, my child?
Your life has just begun.
How did you miss your way so soon
On the course you must run?

You are so young and innocent
You don't even know what life's about.
You followed others down the path
That only brought you heartache, no doubt.

Your friends were all around you
When the booze and drugs flowed free.
Now you're the one paying the price.
Just where might those friends be?

Stop now before it's too late.
Turn around the other way.
Don't let your life end up like those
Who let drugs lead them astray.

Look around my child
At the faces surrounding you here.
The pain, the scars, the hurt
But most of all the fear.

The fear of facing tomorrow,
Without that fix or shot.
Is this where you want to be?
It's where you're headed, like it or not.

There is only one person
To restore the innocence of youth.
And He's always there for you
Even knowing all your truth.

Keep your eyes upon the cross
And you will never lose.
With Christ as your hope and guide
He's the best friend you will ever choose

DAY #112   MISS LOUISE

On Saturday night word soon spread that one of our own, Miss Louise, suffered a stroke and was in serious condition. Miss Louise had recently been transferred to another prison. By Sunday morning we learned just how serious her condition really was. Blood was accumulating on her brain. She was in stable but critical condition.

After breakfast, about seventy-five percent of the dorm gathered in a prayer circle to pray for Miss Louise.

Miss Louise had become DOC and been transferred out of C Dorm shortly after I arrived. All I remember of her is how she continually sat on her bed, speaking to almost no one. That image amazed me even more when I was told why this saintly looking older lady was spending her later years behind bars.

From what I was told, Miss Louise was living with a man on a roommate only situation. He demanded the ten dollars that he had lent her or she could trade the debt for sex. She left and went across the street to collect on a debt from another man. When he refused her collection attempts, she set his house on fire and then went back home to settle her score with her roommate with a knife. She was charged with voluntary manslaughter and ordered to serve twenty-five years. At her age, she would probably never see the outside of the prison gates again.

In all my time here I had never heard such silence. Even during the night you always could hear a toilet flush or faint whispers rising from one point or another.

The deafening silence was only broken by one of the ladies reading James 5:1.

"And the prayer of faith shall save the sick, and the Lord shall raise him up; and if he have committed sins, they shall be forgiven him."

Even those not in the circle, sparsely scattered throughout the dorm, stopped what they were doing. After several short prayers someone started the Lord's Prayer and "everyone" joined in.

As the circle disbanded, several were singing, "I know a prayer will change a thing, will change a thing for me and you."

My evening prayer: "Thank you, Father, for being there for us to come to in our times of trial. Thank you, that prayer is the great equalizer between all of us; that our prayers are heard by You, equally, whether we are a great evangelist or a lowly prisoner. Thank you for the opportunity to come together, no matter what our skin color, or religious denomination, to petition for another one of your precious souls."

* God heard the prayers of this band of prison inmates and spared Miss Louise. Even though the doctors had no hope and vowed she wouldn't live 'til morning, prayer did change a thing. The last I heard is that she is recovering at a state prison hospital, where she will spend her final years, comfortably.

DAY #114   WANTING TO GO HOME

Daily Blessing – *Matthew 11:28-30: Come unto me, all ye that labour and are heavy laden, and I will give you rest.*
29: Take my yoke upon you, and learn of me; for I am meek and lowly in heart: and ye shall find rest unto your souls.
30: For my yoke is easy, and my burden is light.

This is not the HBO series, OZ, nor is it the Wizard of Oz. If it is, then I've left my ruby slippers at home. I've tried many times clicking my heels together and saying: "There's no place like home, there's no place like home." But, I always open my eyes to find I'm not at home, not in Kansas, but still here.

I feel it must be close to time for me to be leaving because the Lord is preparing my heart. I'm beginning to feel a separation from those around me. Before now I felt a part of the ebb and flow; now I feel I'm being pulled away, alone with only my thoughts and my feelings. I'm getting to the point where I can't seem to relate to anyone else's pains and fears. Oh, Lord, please let me go home!

Another sheep left the fold today. I had to say goodbye to Leslie. Seeing those leave that you've grown close to brings on a flood of emotions. Sad to lose a friend, happy that they are going home, jealous you aren't, intensified frustration over the "legal system." A legal system not based on the truth but on who has the best version of the truth, the most believable version; be it accurate or not.

Even though these friends have left, they've left some kind of a mark behind, either physical or emotional. Lonnie left me a towel and a pair of tennis shoes that remind me of the number of times I'd run to the window to light her cigarette so I could get a "hit." Amber left me her dominoes to remind me of the great times we had playing with them.

Beth left me paper and pens because she enjoyed my writings so much. "Shaky" sent me basic necessities to emphasize that there are those that don't forget you when they get out.

Leslie left me her uniform (much smaller) and much nicer than the one I'd worn for one-hundred-thirteen days so I'd feel better about myself and make a better impression in court. Whether this was their logic behind these gifts or not, I don't know, but these are the memories I will cherish long after this ordeal is over.

The following poem was a compilation of a lot of the people I had gotten to know during my stay at the "Rayville Hilton."

Each verse was designed with at least one person in mind, while several verses described more than one.

The first verse was just an introduction, while the second was pinpointed at Ms. Jo. Ms Jo was just a few months older than me but had the wisdom you could only learn from life and a great faith in God. Her strong faith was evidently what was giving her the ability to cope from day to day. You see, Ms Jo, not only had the sons in jail I mentioned earlier, but a daughter that was dying of aids in a Monroe hospital. Whenever she spoke of any of her children she had a gleam in her eye and a lilt in her voice that just emanated the pride she felt for them, no matter what they had done.

The third verse could have covered more than one of the young girls that passed through these doors but this one was specifically written for Jodie.

Jodie was a young girl of nineteen who learned she was pregnant the day she came to jail. Jodie's joy of her first pregnancy was overshadowed by her probation violation for non-payment of fees and not reporting to her probation officer.

Jodie was a very sweet, almost naive, young girl that got an 18 month sentence, which meant her child would be born while she was in jail. Some family members will get her baby until she gets out. The other day she told me that she was having a girl and her boy friend was still standing by her.

Verse four covers a multitude of inmates from their first DWI through their fourth and fifth.

Verse five is for all those young girls like Beth and my own "step-daughter after the fact," Mandy.

Verse six covers a majority of us in here whether it is for drugs, hot checks, DWI or any other reason the state sees fit to lock us up. Most of us are mothers.

Verse seven is specifically written with two people in mind; Tiffany and Jeanette. Fortunately, Tiffany had a great deal more depth than Jeanette who we aptly nicknamed "Barbi." Her tanning bed body and bleached blonde hair (which she claimed was natural) would soon fade and start to show their "true" colors. She came in claiming to be the "prettiest girl in the dorm." In a couple of months I would be interested to see whether or not she could still make that claim.

Verse eight pertains to several, but mainly me. I trusted someone else too much and when she was cornered she turned on me. Now she is sitting on the outside and I'm the one behind bars.

Verse nine includes truly some of the saddest inmates I've seen during my four months here; the homeless. Shamika comes to mind first because she was one of the first to be released after I came. Shamika, like Miss Callie and others, was being released to the streets with no place to go except possibly a shelter. Miss Callie didn't have the option of a shelter. She had been kicked out of most of the homeless shelters in the Monroe area.

One of the guards had told me that she knew Shamika years ago. She said that she was a very prim and proper younger lady. Her clothes were always clean and starched. Then one day Shamika witnessed the murder of her daughter. Since that day Shamika tried to find the relief from her pain in crack cocaine. This only destroyed her mind.

Verse ten covers quite a few whose spouses or children were in other jails. Verse 11 like verse eight applies mainly to me. I've heard a lot of people say that there are no guilty people in jail. I beg to differ with them. Most everyone here admits to their wrongdoing and very few claim innocence. They do, however, offer excuses as to why they did whatever put them here.

The last verse is the simplest way of saying that no matter how crowded we are, even with all four dorms with each of their 75 beds filled and all six lock down cells overflowing, there is always "room for one more."

ROOM FOR ONE MORE

I've seen of much of late,
In my short time here.
Things that have made me laugh and cry
Things that filled me with fear.

I've seen a mother crying
For her dying child on the outside.
For her sons who are in prison
But still she speaks of them with great pride.

I've seen a girl that's pregnant
With her very first child.
A time for joy and happiness
Brings her only emotions that are mild.

I've seen so many who decided
To drink and drive a car.
Unfortunately their learning the hard way
That one extra drink didn't get them far.

I've seen the young ones
Who's had everything in life.
Only to wander down the wrong path,
The path that leads to strife.

I've seen young mothers with babies
Who should really be at home.
They tried a life of drugging
Now her babies are all alone.

I've seen beautiful young women
Who wanted things they had to take.
Now their beauty will dim and fade
While paying for their mistake.

I've seen those who trusted others
For decisions they should make.
Now the others are off and running
And the charges they must take.

I've seen the lost and homeless
Who've no where else to go.
No family, no friends, societies forgotten
These are the saddest cases I know

I've seen families separated by prisons
Mothers and children, husbands and wives.
Each facing their own time in jail
Having to live separate lives.

Then there are those that are innocent
No crimes have they committed today.
But stuck here like the others
Being treated in just the same way.

There is no end to the heartache
That comes through a jailhouse door.
As long as there's temptation
There will always be room for one more

DAY #116   DISRESPECT

Daily Blessing – 1 *Corinthians 6:20 "For ye are bought with a price: therefore glorify God in your body, and in your spirit, which are God's."*
Ephesians 5:2 "And walk in love, as Christ also hath loved us, and hath given Himself for us an offering and a sacrifice to God for a sweet smiling savior."

One of the things that will pop my cork quicker than anything is the total lack of disrespect that a lot of the women, especially the younger ones, have for their elders This includes other's property, other's rights and most of all, themselves. When you stop and think about it, it really isn't hard to comprehend. It was a lack of respect for the law that put most of them in here.

The phrase, "Your rights end where someone else's begins," has no meaning here. It's who can talk the loudest, play the TV the loudest or any agitation factor, i.e. slamming drawers, popping mattresses, snapping fingers or just any other aggravating noise.

Of course the word "intensification" pops up again in regards to disrespect. Things and actions that wouldn't normally bother me on the outside are usually blown out of proportion by the situation I currently face. I soon learned I wasn't the only one with nerves on edge.

Things like trying to watch a TV show or movie while the people around you are talking loudly is extremely nerve racking. Sometimes just a sarcastic quip or even a look can send tempers flaring. I've even seen a fight break out over a Rice Krispy Treat as well as someone not respecting the privacy of another's drawer and their right not to share the snack.

It was not surprising that these women show so much disrespect for everyone and everything around them because it was obvious they lacked a basic self-worth. *In that way respect and love are so alike. If you can't love yourself you can't truly love anyone else. Likewise, if you can't show respect for yourself, how in the world can you show respect for anyone else.*

Day #117   Survival

Thank God as a child I went through Girl Scouts. It taught me certain survival skills I needed for this place. One week in this place could match any episode of "Survivor."

It's amazing how I've learned to take a package of 12 cookies, a candy bar and a bit of hot chocolate or coffee and make a "jailhouse brownie" or Ramen noodles, a meat stick, chips and a package of squeeze cheese to make a "cell block burrito;" all of this without benefit of a stove or microwave. You simply use hot water, which is also used to take a cold honey bun, and convert it to a warm, fresh treat for mornings where cereal is the only breakfast bill of fare.

When it comes to getting stains out of your uniform there isn't any stain that can stand up to "the mixture." This concoction consists of state soap, state toothpaste and the green wrapper from the state toilet paper, torn in small pieces and whipped together. Application of this mixture is by way of the state furnished toothbrush. State toothpaste on a "zit" overnight will cause it to vanish.

Of course there is another use for the toilet paper wrapper. It makes an almost adequate cigarette paper on Wednesday nights before commissary when the next day all you have is butts left with nothing to "re-roll."

Unfortunately the one ingredient in the wrapper that makes it a must in "the mixture" makes it a little unappealing for cigarette paper. That ingredient is bleach.

The phrase, "Necessity is the mother of invention," never found a better home than jail.

DAY #120   **PSI ORDERED**

Once again I was ordered out of my bed at 4:30 to get ready for court. Today was going to be my chance to plead guilty or innocent. I had all my facts lined up for my attorney. Everything I would need to blow Ms. X out of the water.

I couldn't tell you if I had oatmeal or grits for breakfast, I was so nervous. It seemed like I waited an eternity for the guards to put the shackles on me so that we could leave. Never had I imagined I would be eager to be handcuffed! We were finally ushered to the waiting bus and started what I had hoped was my trip to my eventual freedom.

As we pulled in the parking lot of the courthouse I noticed Ms. X getting out of her Lincoln Town car. I knew it would prove to be an interesting day.

All prisoners must first go to the old prison upstairs before they are brought down to the court room. It seemed like an eternity before my name was called to the fate that awaited me two floors below. Actually it was almost five o'clock before the judge could see me.

My attorney was waiting at the defendants' table for me with the news that he had "visited" with the District Attorney and the best I could be offered was the proposition that a PSI (Pre-sentence Investigation) be ordered. If it came back clean I would be allowed to leave with time served. He said that the DA had gotten Ms. X to agree with those terms. The PSI would take about sixty days, at most.

I asked, "What about clearing my name?" I later learned his reply was standard for most of his clients, as well as the clients of the other Indigent Defenders. "You can go to trial, but with all of the briefs, the court dates, the depositions, it could take three or four years and you will be sitting in jail all of that time or you can take a plea bargain and go home."

I knew that I would have nothing on my PSI, so I reluctantly took the plea bargain. That was my lesson in the American justice system that day; *if you're willing to plea bargain quickly, then you'll get sentenced quickly--within six months. But if you stand and fight, if you say, "No, this is wrong," or, "I want to go to court on this," you can expect to wait a long time. And you can expect to get a much harsher sentence because the criminal justice system is vindictive. They punish you if you decide to stick up for yourself.*

No one ever sees a lawyer until 30 seconds before they see the judge because the public defenders are so overburdened. But they are very active in trying to talk people into plea-bargaining. If everyone today asked for their constitutional right to a trial, the system would grind to a halt. *Most plead guilty, whether they are guilty or not. The few who do go to trial usually have lawyers appointed by the state and usually are convicted.*

As much as I knew in my heart that God had everything under control, my mind couldn't help but be skeptical as to how all of this was going to turn out.

My evening prayer: "Lord, more than ever, tonight, my life and my fate are in your hands. I promised you four months ago I would go where You wanted and do what You wish, without questioning. Lord, I know you have a master purpose and a master plan for my life and I entrust it to You. Lord, all I ask is, please, give me the strength I need to face each day of my remaining time and keep reminding me, in whatever way You must, that You are taking each step right with me. Thank you, Father, for going this far with me and not forsaking me."

DAY #122   CYCLES OF JAIL

Elizabeth Kubler-Ross says there are four stages of death. These stages are denial, anger, bargaining, and depression. The same can be said of imprisonment. After all it is the death of your freedom. I've seen it so many times in so many ways in all of the new girls that come in and it all translates the same.

Normally, the first few days are spent in tears, especially the real young ones. "This is not happening to me." This was followed by denial of what they did or might have done. I actually heard one girl on the phone telling her mother "I've done nothing wrong." There was a brief pause while her mother must have started a questioning session. "Yes, Mama, I had a baggie of weed and a pipe." Pause. "Yes, I had a couple of rocks but I wasn't bothering anybody. I didn't do anything wrong."

Then progressively the anger starts to build. Usually the anger is directed toward someone else, the person who informed on them, the cops, or even God.

This anger gives ways to depression. "I can't bear going through this and putting my family through this." In my one-hundred plus days here I've seen this depression take many forms. There was a young girl of nineteen who tried to use an aluminum pie pan from a pecan pie bought on the commissary to cut her wrist because she was so depressed over being in jail.

The prison system is prepared for this phase of the jail cycle, better than any other. There are in every prison, rooms that are called "suicide watch." At Rayville, there was a room directly next to the interlock. It had one bed and one toilet, sink combination. The occupant can be seen by the guard on duty in the interlock at all times. When the inmate is put on "suicide watch" she is not allowed to have anything in her cell. Depending on the severity of the case she might or might not be issued a mattress. Her uniform is taken from her and she is placed in a paper gown, much like the ones the hospitals use. The inmate is left in "suicide watch" until the nurse on duty feels that the inmate is no longer a threat to herself or others.

I have only seen one other girl put on suicide watch since I have been here. That was a girl whose attorney had plea bargained for 5 years on an involuntary manslaughter charge in the death her 4 or 5 year old nephew. When she went to court for the sentence to be pronounced, the judge changed his mind and she got life without possibility of parole on 2nd degree murder charges. I know that kind of betrayal would have put me in suicide watch.

After a while we are all lulled into a sense of acceptance; acceptance of the fact that we are here and will be here for quite a while. This is when we all must decide to either do our time or let our time do us.

The hope for the future through God got some of us through all of the depression.

I had thought a great deal about what emotions I had been through and what I'd learned since I'd been here. After watching and thinking about others I'd seen come and go I realized we all went through the same "cycle."

THE CYCLE OF JAIL

I've had to learned so many things
During my brief stay of sorrow.
But most of all, with God's help
I've learned to handle my fear and horror.

I've come full cycle,
Since my first day here
I've served my time and got the word
That now the end is near.

The cycle began for me
My first night in this place.
I was scared and so afraid
Those around could see it on my face.

Then came the denial,
God wouldn't do this to one so true.
But God didn't put me here for what I'd done
But, for what I could do.

Next were thoughts that surely my family
Would hurry and bail me out.
I knew this deep in my soul
With me there was no doubt.

Once again I was disappointed
That dream was not to come true.
God, I know You are showing me
All I have to do is lean on You.

After the fear, denial and hope past
I learned to accept my fate in stride.
Even guiding and teaching the new ones
Was a job I handled with pride.

Then the ones I became close to,
Started to leave one by one.
I was happy they were going home
But sad I had to be left alone.

The hardest day I ever faced
The day my world was torn apart.
Was when they took my best friend and mentor
It was if they ripped out my heart.

Friendship here are fleeting
And you have to toughen up your heart
A lesson I wished I had learned
Right from the very start.

Now that I am leaving
Some of the old fears return
My world outside has turned upside down
How to live in it, I must learn.

But through the last few months
My faith in God has grown strong.
I know as long as I let Him guide me
He will keep me from all wrong.

DAY #124   PRISONER'S PRAYER

Daily Blessing – *Ecclesiastes 9:10 "Whatsoever thy hand findeth to do, do it with thy might; for there is no work, nor device, nor knowledge, nor wisdom, in the grave, whither thou goest."*

Holly thought it might be a good idea to change the nightly prayer because she said several others were tired of hearing the same one over and over. She read a long complicated prayer that Nanette had received from a friend. It touched me, especially when it referred to the forgiveness of self. That seems to be the biggest obstacle some of these women in here must face, self-forgiveness for not only hurting themselves but all the family and friends affected by their imprisonment.

The Lord allowed me to express it, this way:

PRISONER'S PRAYER

Lord, I come to you tonight
With this my heart felt prayer.
No matter what I've done in my life
I know you're always there.

First, I thank you, Lord
For all that you have done.
For helping me through another day
But most of all for sending Your Son.

These locks and chains that confine me
May keep me from the world, it's true.
But by Your mighty grace and power,
Will never keep me from You.

As I go through tomorrow, Lord.
I ask for You to see me through.
That every thought, word and deed
Will only glorify You.

I pray for my family, Oh Lord.
Help them live with what I've done.
Let them find your comfort and peace
Through Jesus Christ Your Son.

I pray for all my fellow inmates
Within these secured walls.
I pray for your blessings and wisdom
On the guards in the halls.

And now, dear Lord,
My prayer is almost through.
I've only have one thing left
For this sinner to ask of You.

I've done a lot of wrong things
That put me in this place.
Please teach me to forgive myself
Through Your almighty grace.

And now I close my eyes in peace
Free of guilt and shame.
And ask that You accept this prisoner's prayer
All in Jesus' name.

After I wrote that prayer, I realized that I had accepted
the gift of writing from God but I had not fully consecrated
it for His glory. The following prayer I wrote and taped

inside my Bible so that I would never forget from Whom I received my gift and why.

MY WRITER'S PRAYER

Lord, put me in the center of Your will
And help me not depart.
Guide my hand throughout the day
To write what You put on my heart.

Help me touch one life today
To point at least one soul to You.
Let me see there is a purpose
In the writings that I do.

Don't let me hide my talent
Or seek any credit for me.
Help me use it to Your glory
And to magnify only Thee.

And when I lay my pen down at night
My writing for the day is through
Let me have the calm assurance
I couldn't have done it without You.

* From that day until I left Richland Parish Detention Center, I read that prayer every morning and every night. Even though I committed it to memory a long time ago I still feel it necessary to read the words on the page just as my heart had spoken them to God on that first night I committed it to paper.

DAY #126   A SPECIAL MOTHER'S LOVE

On Sunday, I heard a sermon on Mary and all that she went through as the mother of Christ. It made me stop and grasp just what an enormous burden God had put on such a young child, and how she had willingly accepted the challenge and stuck with it to the very end.

I couldn't help but stop and think about my own mother and how she had totally turned her back on me. I quickly came to the realization that if ever there was a perfect blueprint for a mother, Mary was it.

A SPECIAL MOTHER'S LOVE

A young girl of thirteen
Who was to be married one day.
Had a visit from an angel.
Here's what the angel had to say.

"Even though you're still a virgin"
"You are to have a Son"
A child of God and not man
With God He will be One.

This child you are carrying
Will need a special mother,
For He will grow to change the world
This child is like no other.

When He is born the skies will change
And give birth to a star.
Shepherds and kings will journey to see Him
From near and from far.

You will love and nurture Him
For such a very short span
Then He must go and do His Father's work
This is all in God's plan.

His life will not be an easy one
One that no mother would chose.
Though His life will be hard,
His faith He'll never lose.

You must watch Him toil
As He preaches God's word.
And face the pain and ridicule
Where ever He is heard.

Then one day while still a young man
This child will break your heart.
Not with anything He has done
You must know this from the start.

For those He came to save
Will nail Him to a tree.
All because the Son of God
He professes to be.

And you will stand at the foot of the cross
Watching His life's blood flow
Feeling every pain and stripe
This child of yours will know.

You will watch Him die
On that cruel tree
With the sins of all mankind
For all the world to see.

You will watch them
Put Him in the tomb.
And love and curse the day
You carried Him in your womb.

And when His tomb you visit
At the end of the third day
A miracle you will witness
For the stone will be rolled away.

Your Son will not be there
He will be risen from the dead.
Please listen and remember
Every word I've said.

So my child, you've been chosen
By God from up above
To bring this Savior to the world
And show the world a special mother's love.

Day #128   Visit To The Big Yard

Daily Blessing: *Matthew 6:28 "Consider the lilies of the field, how they grow; they toil not, neither do spin."*

Ms. Jesse, the supervisor, promised a dorm-wide shakedown today, so we were all ordered out to the big yard. There were several other dorms already "on the yard" when we arrived. There were two teams playing volleyball but most of the inmates were either watching the game or visiting with friends. I sat down in a shady spot on the grass and started to read my Bible.

The sun was so bright that I took a moment to shield my eyes and that's when I saw it; an incredibly small flower pushing its way through the mortar between the bricks of one of the dorm walls.

God never ceases to amaze me. Even though I've put my complete trust in Him, there are times I find myself losing hope, but God always comes through even if it's as simple as sending a little flower to remind me to never give up.

A SIGN OF HOPE

Today while out on the prison yard
I saw a most peculiar sight.
A small little wildflower
Coming through the bricks with all its might.

I though just how significant
That flower was to me.
It made me realize
Something I needed to see.

The flower was like my life,
Struggling all the way.
Pushing through the hard times
That come along every day.

The three strong leaves
Coming off a stem of one.
Signified the Holy Trinity;
The Holy Spirit, the Father, and the Son.

The leaves nurture and support
This tiny little flower.
Giving it light and moisture
To create its own power.

That flower had such determination
To make it through that wall.
How shameful and guilty I felt
To think that God would let me fall.

So, thank you Lord
For all that You do,
Especially showing me that little flower
As a sign of hope from You.

DAY #129   NICKIE

A young lady who came in several days prior to my writing this poem proved to be the inspiration. Several ladies in the dorm had approached me and asked me to remember her in special prayer. It seemed she did not believe in God.

I later found out from one of the guards that she had once been an extremely beautiful model who served a short stay here a couple of years earlier. When she returned this time, a guard recognized her and noticed how her skin had become very ruddy, her hair bleached to straw, and her weight had dropped to eighty or eighty-five pounds. The guard asked her if the drug use was worth it. She answered, "Ever minute of it."

HE STILL BELIEVES IN YOU

I turned my back on God
For all I thought He'd done wrong.
For letting wars and violence claim young lives
And ignoring the hungry, homeless throng.

I looked all over for the answer
For why God could let these things be.
And after years of begging,
I was sure He couldn't hear me.

So, I turned my face to God
And He finally answered me:
"I did not bring evil in this world"
"I sent My Son to set men free."

"When I created man"
"I gave him free will"
"And some decisions he made long ago"
"Are affecting mankind, still."

"I know I could not change"
"What man was set to do."
"But I could send a Comforter"
"To help him make it through."

So, if you turn your back on God
And say His existence isn't true,
Even though you don't believe in Him
He still believes in you.

DAY #130   SONDRA

Sondra lost her younger brother to a heart attack while she was in here. She and I talked about how close knit her mother and her brother were. Sondra asked me to write a poem for her mother about her brother. This was what the Lord gave me.

A MOTHER AND A SON'S LOVE

There is a star in heaven
That sings your praise above
To God and all His angels
For you're a perfect example of a mother's love.

You loved us all
In our own special way,
But God needed another star
And took your son away.

No one knows the hurt and anguish
No one really know the loss,
Except God, our Father,
Who sent His Son to die on the cross.

Your arms ache to hold him,
To dry His tears away.
And God has made the promise
You'll do that again, someday.

You want to talk to Him
To tell him about your day.
But when you reach for the phone
You have to turn away.

God created a special connection
Between a mother and a son,
Sometimes without realizing it
You think and act as one.

So draw on that connection.
Look to the stars above.
Speak to that star that sings your praise
It's your son, the brightest star above.

My evening prayer – *"Father, thank you for showing me that no matter how we feel our problems and our pain are unique to us, there are always others with hurts so deep only You can reach down and comfort their aching heart."*

* Almost 8 months later I copied it and gave it to Ms Parnell at lunch with several other poems I had written. There was no particular reason on my part, other than that she had become very interested in my writing and I had copied several for her.

That night at supper she asked me why I had written that poem for her. I told her that I hadn't written it for her. She said she had also lost her son, and it was very close to the anniversary of his death. She thought the poem was so appropriate because her son was her whole world.

Later that night another guard, Ms. Woolsey, woke me and asked for a copy because she too had lost her son and felt it really spoke to her.

DAY #136   **WHAT KIND OF BIBLE ARE YOU?**

Daily Blessing – *Matthew 5:16 "Let your light so shine before men, that they may see your good works, and glorify your Father which is in heaven."*

As a "pre-trial" dorm, C Dorm was very transitory. As many as 5 or 6 prisoners could leave on a daily basis, only to be replaced by others. Some of the inmates were parish prisoners, serving their time for misdemeanor offenses of prostitution, simple possession, public intoxication or just plain loitering. The rest of us were just sitting and waiting for our chance in court or to be sentenced.

Most of the inmates that had inhabited these beds when I first arrived were now gone, either to other dorms or home and the "quality" of the dorm was diminishing by leaps and bounds. More and more I was beginning to see a lot more thievery and total disrespect for rules and authority. The worse part of it was those most guilty were the main ones running to church and leading prayers in prayer groups.

I prayed for the Lord to send me something that would wake them up. He reminded me of something my mother had taught me as a child. *"Your life is the only Bible some people will ever read."*

WHAT KIND OF BIBLE ARE YOU?

Your life is the only Bible
Some people will ever read.
How many of us live each day
So others to Christ we might lead?

What book and what chapter
Did someone read today?
Was it Exodus and the Ten Commandments,
And was it read the right or wrong way?

How about the words from your mouth?
Did they edify God,
Or just put another stumbling block
On the path others must trod?

How about Christ's only commandments
Did you leave them on the shelf?
Love God with all your heart
And your neighbor as yourself.

Did you live the Great Commission,
The only thing Christ commanded us to do;
To teach and preach His story
In words and actions, too.

So, look back upon this day,
The things you've done and said.
What kind of Bible through you
Have other people read?

DAY #143   EASTER

It is no surprise that holidays are especially tough in prison. When you lose a loved one around one of the holidays it only intensifies the loss. Scarlet lost her mother shortly before Easter.

As I prayed with her and tried to counsel her with the words the Lord put on my heart, I couldn't help but think about my own father's death and what he might have to say if he could speak to me.

DINING WITH THE SAINTS THIS YEAR

As you gather together this Easter
It will be the first without me.
Don't feel so lost and all alone,
For each of your faces I can see.

I know that you are missing me,
I feel your pain and fear.
Don't worry about me this Easter
I'll be dining with Jesus and the saints this year.

I see your grief and sorrow
And hear each tearful moan.
But God has reassured me
He hasn't left you alone.

So love and keep each other
As Jesus commanded you to do.
'Cause I can see the many blessings
He has ready to pour out on you.

This is a time of year for rejoicing
So try and not be sad, my dear
Don't worry about me this Easter
I'll be dining with Jesus and the saints this year.

I sent you a special Easter gift
From my Heavenly home above.
Every time you see an Easter Lily
It will be a sign of my undying love.

Heaven's such a beautiful place,
With old friends and loved ones near.
So don't worry about me this Easter
I'll be dining with Jesus and the saints this year.

The banquet table is all set
At the head our risen King.
The air is filled with praises
As the heavenly angels sing.

I find my seat at the table
Amongst the heavenly throng
I close my eyes in amazement
While I join in their sweet song.

The hope of Easter is Christ is living
And promises life eternal for all
All we have to do is just believe
And He'll be there should we stumble and fall.

When your time comes to join us
And you stand at the gate so forlorn.
I'll smile and gently ask you
"My dear, what took you so long."

DAY #144   WHAT I LEARNED DURING THIS TIME

Daily Blessing – *Jeremiah 29:11 "For I know the thoughts that I think toward you, saith the LORD, thoughts of peace, and not of evil, to give you an expected end."*

I am all too aware of the mission field the Lord placed me on 144 days ago. Although, I think that "placed me in" would be a more suitable term. In so many ways He has shown me that I was here to learn and then put what He taught me into action.

I guess for my education to be more effective I need to summarize what I've learned up to this point.

The first things He has helped me understand are the people around me and why they are here. The most common type of crime that women have been imprisoned for in recent years is violation of laws prohibiting the possession or sale of drugs. Women are rarely imprisoned for violent crimes and much less so than incarcerated men.

There are no big time gangsters here, no premeditated mass murderers; no godmothers. There are no big time dope dealers, no kidnappers; no Watergate women. There are virtually no women here charged with white-collar crimes such as embezzling or fraud. Most of the women have drug related cases. Many are charged as accessories to crimes committed by men. The major crimes that women here are charged with are prostitution, pick pocketing, shop lifting, robbery and drugs. Women who have prostitution cases or who are doing "fine" time make up a substantial part of the short- term population. The women see stealing or hustling as necessary for the survival of themselves or their children because jobs are scarce and welfare is impossible to live on.

For many, prison is not very different from the street. It is, for some a place to rest and recuperate. For the prostitute, prison is a vacation from turning tricks in the rain and snow. It can be a vacation from brutal pimps. Prison for the addict is a place to get clean, get medical work done and gain weight. Often, when the habit becomes too expensive, the addict gets herself busted, (usually subconsciously) so she can get back in shape, leave with a clean system, ready to start all over again. One woman claimed that for a month or two every year she either goes jail or to the "crazy house" to get away from her husband.

God has also showed me the value of true friendship and how if we just open our eyes we will see He sends them freely. He has allowed so many wonderful, interesting and fascinating people to travel this leg of my journey with me.

Some came into my life for a reason. It was usually to meet a need I had expressed to Him, either outwardly or inwardly. They had come to assist me through a difficulty, to provide me with guidance and support, to aid me physically, emotionally, or spiritually. They may seem like a Godsend, and they are. They are there for the reason I needed them to be. Then, without any wrongdoing on either one's part or at an inconvenient time, the relationship would end. Sometimes they are transferred. Sometimes they walk away. Sometimes they act-up or out and force you to take a stand. What I must realize is that my need has been met, my desire fulfilled; their work is done. The prayer I sent up has been answered and it is now time to move on.

Then there were those people that came into my life for a season, because my turn had come to share, grow, and learn. They might have brought me an experience of peace or made me laugh. They sometimes taught me to do something I have never done. They always gave me an unbelievable amount of joy. Believe it! It is real, but only for a season. They, too, had to depart so I could continue my journey.

Finally, God sent very special friends to teach me lifetime lessons. Those things I needed to build upon in order to have a solid emotional and spiritual foundation. I had to learn to accept these lessons, love the person involved; and put what I have learned to use in all other relationships, and areas of my life. These extraordinary people made such an impression on my life and my heart that it was obvious the seed of friendship was planted by God, Himself.

I think the best way I can express my appreciation to all of these friends is *"You came into my life for a reason, stayed for a season but left your mark for a lifetime."*

THE SEED OF FRIENDSHIP

Did God ever send you something
That you never knew you needed?
You didn't have to ask Him for it
Let alone, never even pleaded.

In one of my darkest hours
When I didn't know what to do
God already had planted the seed of friendship
Deep within the heart of you.

For He knew that soil was fertile
And rich in all it would need
To create all the fruits of a loving friendship
From that tiny little seed.

That seed was warmed by the sunshine
Of your incredible smile.
And then watered by your caring tears
Every once in a while.

And when storms of doubt and fear
Threatened the safety of that seed
Your unending trust and confidence
Provided the shelter it would need.

That seed may have been planted by God
But your love and nurturing is what made it grow
Into one of the deepest, abiding friendships
I would ever come to know.

As thankful as I am for each of these extraordinary women that traveled some part of this journey with me, I must say the greatest friendship I made was with the best friend I'll have, not only the rest of my life, but throughout eternity. That is my Lord and Savior, Jesus Christ because of what He did for me.

"Greater love hath no man than this, that a man lay down his life for his friends" John 15:13

PART II
TIME FOR GROWTH

DAY #146   CHURCH GOING & WORSHIPING

Church-going and worshiping God can prove to be an interesting observation in prison.   There are as many different reasons for going to church as there are inmates that go. The first and foremost reason for church attendance should be to worship and praise God. It is impossible and against scripture to judge what is one's motivation for what they do, especially in reference to the Lord and His service but sometimes the reasons are so apparent that judgment is not necessary. Some make it very obvious that their primary reason for church attendance is to visit some of the inmates from the other dorms or to just "get out" of their particular dorm for more than just a meal.

For those with alternative motives, it is important to learn which particular ministry is coming which particular day. Some of the ministries are known for handing out goodies, especially around holiday time and it is important to know which group is likely to bring the best favors.

One certain female that was notorious for sleeping as late as she could each day was suddenly spurned into making sure everyone was not only awake and up but also that each and every bed was made and the dorm was clean. This is not because of any great pang of conscience, but because Ms. Carter will not allow the "church ladies" to come into the dorm unless it is spotless. We all knew they would be bringing an appealing bag of treats which turned out to be an attractive plastic cross on a string which was the same color as the cross. This extremely nice gesture was met with snide remarks from some because it wasn't cookies, candy or just more.

The reason I do not attend church is not because of these ladies attitude or hidden agendas.   I'm reminded of something that a former pastor once told my father when he was in a similar situation with fellow churchgoers.

Brother Penell asked Daddy if he would rather, "sit in the pews with them on Sunday or burn in hell with them forever?"

My own apprehension in trying to attend worship with these ladies is that my low distraction level keeps me from being able to devote my full concentration on the worship.

I feel that I can get much closer to God in my bunk in a one on one experience with Him in a much more peaceful setting as time and environment will allow.

DAY #153   EASTER LETTER TO MAMA

It has now been over five months since I've heard from Mama. I try not to think about it but it does creep into my mind on occasion. The worst part is the loneliness. I want to share so much with her of what I've experienced but I feel I would only waste my postage. I've got a collection of letters that I've written to, hopefully, give her someday. If not in this lifetime, she will be able to read them from my heart when she goes to be with the Lord.

I thought I'd use the letter I wrote Mama for my Easter thoughts this year.

> *Dear Mama,*
>
> *I am about to celebrate one of the greatest holidays that Christendom observes each year and that is Easter; the day our Lord rose from the grave He willingly allowed Himself to be placed in so He could take on my sins, however hideous they might be.*
>
> *When I think of all the miseries I have faced these last months I must say that they pale when put in the light of what Christ did for me. I soon realize I have nothing to complain about but just should only be thankful to God that I can celebrate the glory of Christ this Easter because I know now what Christ went through and He faced every torment and torture for me.*
>
> *Every year, up until now, I have made sure that you had a lily at Easter. I apologize that I won't be able to continue that tradition this year so I've tried to do the next best thing. I'm sending you a poem about the lily.*

THE LILY

A single lily once grew
In a lonely barren field.
The field lay in a valley
At the foot of a hill.

The lily was very sad and lonely
As it sat in the field one day.
'Til a bee came along and said:
"Our Heavenly Creator sent me your way."

"He said that your nectar"
"Is the sweetest ever known"
"He wants me to spread your seeds"
"So you won't have to stand alone."

The lily held it's head up high
As it beamed with pride.
Because it didn't take long
For others to grow by it's side.

One day the lily noticed
A group of people on the hill.
He heard the birds whispering
They had taken someone there to kill.

Soon there appeared a woman
Who plucked the lily from where it grew.
Through the tears on her face appeared a smile
As she whispered "I'm so glad I found you."

"Out of all the flowers here"
"You are surely the one."
"The most perfect lily of the valley"
"For the tomb of my most perfect Son."

She lovingly carried the lily
And placed it by Her dead Son.
Even though the lily knew he would die
He felt honored to be the chosen one.

He lay there several days
And suddenly noticed a bright light.
For the Son that was dead
Stood up with all His might.

He picked up the lily
And held it to His chest.
"You shall be the flower to herald my resurrection;"
"Chosen among all the rest."

"Because you were faithful"
"And did as your Creator bid you to."
"You gave your life to comfort another"
"That's why I've chosen you."

From that day forward the Easter lily
Symbolizes the day Christ rose.
To tell how much Christ loved us
Every where the lily grows.

May God bless you and keep you this Easter as you celebrate the glory of Christ and may He always keep you in His care.

Love always,
Your daughter, Tracey

DAY #155   ELIZABETH

Daily Blessing – *I John 3:17 "But whoso hath this world's good, and seeth his brother have need, and shutteth up his bowels of compassion from him, how dwelleth the love of God in him?"*

When Elizabeth joined our ranks a couple of days ago, the gossip started right away. She had been brought in and on charges of child abuse. Not her own child but a friend's child. She had been accused of binding the child, who I believe was 3 or 4, in duct tape and putting him in a doghouse to punish him. These particular charges made her very unpopular with the rest of the dorm. Any charges that have to do with harming or killing a child would be all that the women needed to ostracize that particular inmate. This particular young lady also had some peculiar habits that disturbed those around her. A lot of the girls in the dorm started saying she was a Satanist.

I began praying that the Lord would open a door because I was at a loss as how to begin the conversation without making her angry. Then I remembered something that a preacher had said years ago. When he was asked about approaching people with the good news of Christ, how did he do it without running them off? He replied: "Where are you going to run them to, a deeper hell?"

I noticed that she was sitting on her bunk writing, so I walked over and simply asked if I could talk to her for a moment. At first she seemed very surprised because so few had given her even one kind word. I simply asked her one question that seemed to throw her off guard for a moment. I asked her if she was a Satanist that followed the teachings of Anton La Vey or was she Wiccan.

My daughter, Catherine, had become involved in the Wiccan system of belief, so I had studied it to arm myself with the knowledge I needed to show her where that particular "religion" falls short of what Christ teaches. Never did I realize that I would ever use that knowledge again. Once again the Lord prepared me long before I needed it.

Her eyes lit up and her mouth dropped open in astonishment. She proceeded to tell me that she didn't realize anyone in here would have any concept as to what Wiccan was. Now I had the information I needed, she was Wiccan. She also told me that she, her mother and aunt were "chosen ones." That means that they believed they were born with special powers of witchcraft.

I knew then, that the Lord had really given me quite an assignment this time, but I also knew He would be right there with me, guiding me in everything I said, if I just let Him. I knew that was not the time to come down on her with all of the fallacies of her religion. I had to take some time to get my head together and do some studying in the Bible.

One thing our brief talk did was to get me to thinking what my God was to me.

WHAT GOD IS TO ME

I once was asked a question:
"What God is to me?"
I had to ponder on this a while
So the answer I could fully see.

First of all, He's my Creator,
The Supreme Being that made me.
And then He is my Father
Without Him I would not be.

He is my Teacher and my Counselor
Of all things great and small.
His knowledge fills and sustains me
With me He shares it all.

He is my Confidant and Friend
With Him I can talk at length.
About my joys, about my sorrows
His friendship give me strength.

He is my Good Shepherd,
Eager to show me the way.
No matter where I might wander
Anytime of the night or day.

He is my Provider,
He supplies all I need.
Just by resting in His promise
To the manna He will lead.

He is my Comforter
Whenever grief comes along.
He knows how to lift my spirit
And fill my heart with song.

He is my Great Physician
He heals my body and my heart.
Even when I don't know the problem
He knows just where to start.

And when I've done wrong
He is my Judge on high
Tempering His justice with mercy
To draw me ever nigh.

But if I have to answer
What the greatest thing He might be
I'd have to say my Savior and Lord
Because He willingly died for me.

So He is the Alpha and Omega
The Beginning and the End.
And even if there were no Heaven
I'm glad on earth, He's my Best Friend.

DAY #156   MIXED NUTS

I have now officially renamed my area of the dorm to, "the Forrest Gump area," because we have more than our share of "mixed nuts." Some real, some that put up the façade to scare everyone off so that they won't have to be bothered with other people.

One of the most difficult things to overcome is the noise. Seventy-four plus voices speaking at once, struggling to be heard over all the rest and a television cranked to its highest level. It took me quite awhile to realize the never-ending chatter for some was their own escape. *If they were talking, they weren't thinking. If they weren't thinking, they weren't feeling. If they weren't feeling, they didn't have to face the reality and pain of their situation.*

DAY #157   **JOY OF THE LORD**

Today is the day the Lord has shown me that I need to start talking to Elizabeth. I knew that it wasn't going to be easy but this is what the Lord showed me that I needed to teach her.

The Wiccan faith is not a Christian faith, nor can it be combined in any way, shape or form to enhance the Christian Gospel. Christianity cannot be used to enhance Wiccan, either. Matthew 6:24 says *"No man can serve two masters; for either he will hate the one and love the other; or else he will hold to the one and despise the other. You cannot serve God and mammon."*

Christ's Gospel is not inclusive of any other form of worship or belief. God established this in the first commandment, *"Thou shalt have no other gods before me."* *Exodus 20:3.*

Wiccans advocate that any religion, or combination of religions, is the way to heaven and God. This is contradicted by quite a few scriptures in the Bible such as Ephesians 2:8 – "For by grace that we are saved, through faith; and that not of yourselves; it is the gift of God."

Of course for her to accept those ideas she would have to accept the Bible. I had to be ready with a philosophical approach if she didn't acknowledge the infallibility of the Bible. I had it. Wicca says that they accept the religion of Christianity, but reject the principle that Jesus Christ is the only way to heaven. There was the contradiction I needed. You cannot accept Christianity without accepting its foundational precept that teaches that faith in Christ is the only way to heaven. I had to convince her that this contradiction in itself is illogical, unreasonable, irrational and idiotic.

Normally, in the free world, when I was confronted with a question or a situation such as this I would go to my computer and research the World Wide Web. Here I was with no computer, no web, not even a reliable library with books that I could use for research. All I had was my Bible and the Holy Spirit. I soon learned that was all I needed.

I had several talks with Elizabeth and just as I was about to get her to see the fallacies of Wiccan, she would get a letter or visit from her mother and I'd face a set back. I will say that through all of this she never turned me off or turned me down. She always listened and respected what I had to say.

One day after one of our discussions she asked me to read some of her poetry. She had read quite a bit of mine and valued my opinion. I found it so dark, depressing and death centered. I told her that she didn't seem to be getting the joy from her religion that she should. I wrote this to show where my joy came from.

THE JOY OF THE LORD

"The joy of the Lord is my strength"
The prophet Nehemiah had to say.
And this was before the Messiah's coming
Think how much greater it is today.

Before I found my Savior,
I was as cynical as could be.
Finding fault with everything
When the greatest fault was within me.

When my weeping
Has endured all through the night
He brings me joy in the morning
With a new days shining light.

They say your greatest joy
Is measured by your deepest grief.
When I feel the pain He suffered for me
The joy of His love is way beyond belief.

There's joy in the knowledge
That where ever I am I'm free.
For where there's the Spirit of the Lord
There is always true liberty.

The greatest joy of all
The Lord ever bestowed on me
Was the day I accepted Him as my Savior
And ensured my joy for eternity.

Too many times we Christians like to preach about the joy of our salvation but how often do we really show it?

DAY #158   END OF NICKIE'S STORY

Daily Blessing – *Philippians 4:4 "Rejoice in the Lord always: and again I say, Rejoice."*

There was another female that was in our dorm that I had been told didn't believe in God. I'll call her by the name, May. I learned that at one time May had been an extremely beautiful woman and a very successful model.

In spite of her physical beauty, May had been born with a physical condition that made her very bitter and she blamed God for her condition. Like many others, she fell into the drug scene that was so prevalent around her, as a temporary escape.

The drugs not only affected her mind and her physical appearance, they also robbed what must have been a beautiful light inside her. Her eyes were cold and dark and had such an empty look about them.

May spoke to no one, nor did she make any friends. I didn't know how to reach her but once again the Lord stepped in and took over.

One night several of the girls set up a talent show to pass the time. Some sang, some told jokes, some did skits. A couple of the girls asked me to read a poem of mine. I had a terrific headache and I told them I couldn't read it but I would let someone else read one. I opened up my book of poetry and it fell to a particular poem. (*The Love Affair*)

The girl that was chosen to read it did a pretty good job of destroying it so I was asked to re-read it. Since God and I wrote it I knew what inflections to insert and when to pause at the right places.

After I finished reading this poem many were clapping but I looked over at May and those once cold, empty eyes had tears in them. As I walked back to my bunk she grabbed my arm and in a voice cracking with emotion she said, "thank you."

I noticed after that night that she started reading her Bible and began reaching out to others.

Later on down the road of my journey I had to leave May and Elizabeth behind but I learned later that May accepted Christ a couple of months later, before she went home. All I can say about Elizabeth is I hope I gave her some food for thought. I pray the next time she is confronted with the Gospel, she'll accept Christ as the one true and only way.

DAY #159   THE DOPE MAN

Some of those in our dorm were going through their own private hell. I guess each of us had thoughts and feelings we never expressed. When issues aren't discussed they manifest themselves many times through nightmares. The Lord put the following poem on my heart and my pen one night after I was awakened by a certain inmate screaming in her sleep. After this was repeated for several nights, I soon discovered that there was only one person in the dorm who knew what made her nightmares so horrific. I happened to stumble upon that inmate and she confided in me. While she was on the streets she would sell her children to the dope man to cover her habit.

My feelings of rage over how a mother could do such a thing began to obsess all of my thoughts. When I asked the Lord for some understanding and some peace with this, He let me know; "Now you are beginning to see the gambit of degradation that drugs can bring into a person's life. Use it."

I started to despise this illusive dope man as I began to wonder just what God had in store for someone that issued nothing but heartache, pain, destruction and death; all for a profit.

HEY MISTER DOPEMAN

Hey Mister Dopeman
How are you today?
No, I don't want to buy anything
I've just got something to say.

I've just spent some time
With several of your friends.
I use that term lightly,
Considering how they met their ends.

That young pregnant girl
You dealt to the other day.
Had her child this morning.
But it won't make it, the doctors say.

That tender boy of fifteen
You "gave" your samples to,
Robbed and killed a man last night,
So he could buy more from you.

A once attractive blonde woman,
You've been dealing to for years,
Slashed her wrist the other day
After looking in the mirror through her tears.

The mother of three you saw,
Who was depressed over a letter,
Has left her children alone on earth.
She figured a little was good, a lot was better.

You deal in pain and destruction,
Those are your primal wares.
And you sell it under the pretense,
Of relieving all their cares.

I came to see your little sister.
She tried the stuff that belonged to you.
She couldn't hear all the "no's" you said,
She was too busy watching what you do.

Like so many of your other victims
I was there for her last breath.
In case I failed to introduce myself
I'm called the "Angel of Death."

One day when it's your turn,
And I shall come for you,
God will look at all you've sent me.
He's the One you'll answer to.

DAY #160   CATHERINE'S VISIT

There was one high point in having my stepdaughter in here with me. Her father, Carl, my ex-husband, came to see her today and brought my daughter, Catherine and my grandson, Christopher. I have never seen a more beautiful sight in my life than those two precious faces. My precious baby was now walking. When I left he was still a babe in arms, now he was becoming a little man. The forty-five minutes we had together was all too short but I couldn't be despondent about anything. All I could do was thank God that they were safe, well, and happy.

The inspiration for this next poem came when I began to have strong feelings that I'd be going home soon. It is hard to explain but I began to feel separated from my surroundings and a feeling that maybe my work was finished or close to finishing. I wanted to thank the Lord for the experience, even though it was very trying and taxing. I felt like this would be my last poem I would write while in prison

As it turned out I was experiencing these feelings of separation so that I could focus better on my writing and what the Lord was trying to have me say. I was becoming too emotionally involved to be objective.

THANK YOU, LORD

Thank you Lord
For sending me to this place.
Even though at first I thought,
Prison would only bring me shame and disgrace.

You put me on a battleground,
Where the devil's a might foe.
There are many battle scars here
On lives that have been brought so low.

You called me to a mission field
With lost souls to be saved.
Where you wanted Your salvation shared
With those who's spent a life to sin enslaved.

You sent me on an humbling journey,
That put me on my knees.
And made me ever mindful
It was You I had to please.

You've placed me here to show me
True Christian fellowship at its best.
That there are those who care about me
When I've been forgotten by the rest.

You've stripped me of all things
That You knew would hinder me,.
The possessions and the people,
That came between me and Thee.

But mainly You sent me here to teach me
Some things I needed to learn.
You put the desire within my heart
For Your will, You made me yearn.

You taught me how to stay
Within a constant state of prayer.
And how to lean on You
For my every need and care.

You taught me, dear Lord
Happiness is not in earthly things.
That true joy is in my salvation.
That's what really should make my heart sing.

You've taught to use the talent
You so graciously gave to me.
And I give all the honor and the glory
To no one else but Thee.

You reminded me how to use the Bible
As the place I needed to go.
When I was presented with a question
And the answer I did not know.

You taught me that forgiveness
Truly begins with me.
And unless I forgive others
How can I ever expect forgiveness from Thee?

I've tried to be an humble servant.
Your will I've tried to do.
How can I complain and moan
For all I've received from You?

But Lord, I am so unworthy
For the work you've chosen me to do.
And, Lord, I never would have made it
Without a lot of help from You.

And when I finally leave this place
I know my job will not be done.
In fact, dear Lord, You have showed me
It's only just begun.

DAY #162   REHABILITATION?

One of the greatest fallacies I've learned while here is that "prison is for rehabilitation." If a prison is for rehabilitation, the inmate must first feel the need to be rehabilitated. Most of them feel they don't need to make any changes; their life is just fine as it is, thank you.

Then there were those that seem to have no conscience, which rendered them incapable of remorse. I had seen it on a lesser level with the common drug dealers and users that couldn't wait to get out and continue what they had been doing to put them here.

Entering prison for the first time can be a frightening experience. The noise level is the first thing that strikes you and it is unlike any noise that you have ever known. There is such a combination of human sounds and clamor that individual and specific noises are almost undecipherable.

Prisoners come from a variety of backgrounds. Prison is a confined place, packed with living bodies of every shape, color and size. There will be times that you find yourself closer to other human beings than you have ever been before and unfortunately many of them you won't like and what's more, they won't like you.

There is a class of people who are "at home" behind prison bars. They have been conditioned since childhood for prison life. They started out in juvenile facilities, moved on to youth reformatories and then hit the big time with adult prisons. To them prison is a controlled, "safe" environment where they are clothed, fed, and told what to do. The outside world is too much of a challenge and too frightening for them.

Another class of people looks at prison as if it were a homeless shelter. It's not that they want to be in prison, but life situations have forced them there. These homeless, unskilled, and destitute women come in on charges of the minor crimes so that they can be guaranteed their "three hots and a cot" while they take a break from their homelessness and drug addiction. These ladies aren't really criminals; they just use the prison system as a way out of their social or economic conditions. And they do it repeatedly..

Then there is the final class of prisoner that is the true criminal. These are the scariest because they make no excuses for their crime and will openly discuss just what they will do once they are released and back on the streets, whether it be gang banging, robbing or peddling dope.

The hardest case I came in contact with was a girl in her early twenties. I was very surprised to learn that she was in for first-degree murder. Within the last few days she and three of her friends had gone to her stepfather's house to buy drugs. While they were there they decided to rob and then kill him. They stabbed and shot him to death. Her crime was not what stunned me but her attitude didn't fit into the normal cycles of jail. She came in laughing, joking and quickly joined in with the young "fun click" that thought they were only there to have a good time.

It was hard for me to understand because had I been in her shoes, I would have been in shock that I had taken a human life. Secondly, I would have been scared to death about my own fate.

I do have to admit that I have met a few who knew their lives had to be changed. There were some that even admitted if they hadn't come to jail they would probably be dead. These are the ones I admired, those that found their purpose for being here. This change was not brought about through anything the prison or prison system did. This change was brought about only through Christ and their acceptance of Him as their Lord and Savior.

DAY #164   PART-TIME CHRISTIANS

I originally wrote this poem in a shorter version but when I read it to Sondra, she came out with the line "God don't like no part-timers." I knew I had to incorporate it in the poem. It was also originally inspired by some of the things I'd seen going on around me.

GOD DON'T LIKE NO PART-TIMERS

God don't like no part-timers
To see His work through.
And if you are one of them
I'm speaking directly to you.

Do you use God as a convenience
Only when you are in need of Him?
If He had the same conviction towards you
You chance of salvation would be slim.

What is Jesus had only journeyed
Half way up to Calvary's hill?
And laid down the cross because it wasn't convenient
It and our salvation would be lying there still.

Do you ever just stop and thank Him
For all He has done?
For the great things and the small things
And especially for sending His Son.

Or do you take God for granted
Until an emergency comes your way?
How would you feel if your children
Treated you like that everyday?

You say you don't feel like serving Him
Each and everyday.
That it's really not important
He's too busy to notice anyway.

God wants us to serve Him
In everything that we do.
Even the smallest lie or sin
Will separate Him from you.

So serve God gladly everyday,
Diligently seek His will for you.
And you won't be a part-timer
But a loyal servant, proud and true.

DAY #169   **GOD'S WILL BE DONE**

Daily Blessing – *Psalm 37:5 "Commit thy way unto the Lord; trust also in Him; and He shall bring it to pass."*

I began to face a period of great frustration over waiting for a court date. I kept praying and claiming but nothing seemed to happen. I received a certain peace when I finally realized that I had not surrendered my situation to the Lord. I was still trying to call the shots. I had to let Him do exactly as He pleased. It was me that had to be in harmony with God's will, not vice versa.

GOD'S WILL BE DONE

I've read every book
On the prison library shelves.
I've seen every movie more than twice
Including one on elves.

I've been to church and read the Bible through,
Looking for Your will to find.
Now there's one thing I'm asking
If you really don't mind.

Please let me go home, Lord.
They said I'd be here a short time.
But that short time has come and gone
And I've truly paid for my crime.

So, let me go home, God
That's in my prayers each night.
I promise with all my heart and soul
Only to do what is right.

I've claimed it, God,
Your promise I'd soon be free.
Now, I'll stop and listen
To what you have to say to me.

Yes, God, I pray each night
That Your will be done.
And, yes, I even mention
In the name of Your Son.

You say You have a purpose
All within Your divine plan.
And the will of You, Oh God
Doesn't always match the will of man.

So, God, what you're telling me
Is there's a reason I am still here.
And what I should be praying
Is for You to make that reason clear.

Now, God, I understand it.
That soon I will be free.
But all within your time frame
Not something decided by me.

So, put my will in harmony with Yours
Help me accept Your will for me.
Then even behind these locks and bars
I know I truly will be free.

DAY #170   MOTHER'S DAY IS FOR DAUGHTERS, TOO

This was the first Mother's Day I was to be separated from my two, dear daughters. I have to admit that I had intermittent thoughts about my own mother but since there still had been no contact, I didn't know if she were alive or dead. All I had to offer for her was a prayer to God that if she were still alive, He'd find someway to let her know I held no animosity toward her and that I still loved her.

I felt compelled to write this next poem to Catherine because she was now a mother, herself. The last verse was something she actually told me in a phone conversation. That one simple sentence summed up a lifetime of, "I must have done something right in raising her." I read it to the dorm on the eve of Mother's Day and dedicated it to all the daughters that couldn't be with their mother's on that special day.

HAPPY MOTHER'S DAY, DAUGHTER

I have a present for you, my daughter
On this very special Mother's Day.
It's nothing I can wrap or bundle
It's just something I have to say.

On the day you were born,
I held you in my arms
Scared to death but committed
To keep you from all harms.

As you grew, I watched you,
Each and every day.
Giving thanks to God,
For sending you my way.

I wanted so many things,
For my precious little girl.
And if I could have, sweetheart
I would have given you the world.

I'd pray each night
For the right things to say and do.
To instill just the right values
God would want in you.

Now you are grown
And my work is done.
You've got a little one of your own
Your work has just begun.

I see now all the nights of worry
All the prayers at length.
Were all worth it in the end
Because you became my tower of strength.

And the one day I'll most remember,
Was the day I expressed my pride so true.
You just smiled and replied
"But, Mama, I got it all from you."

As in the title, this poem was written and sent to my
precious daughter, Kira, to let her know how privileged I
felt to be her mother even though I didn't give birth to her.
When Kira was very small she saw my Caesarean scar from

Catherine's birth. That was when she told me, "Catherine was born in Mama's tummy and Kira was born in Mama's heart." I don't think the greatest philosopher could have said it any better.

HAPPY MOTHER'S DAY, KIRA

You may not have been born from me
But you are mine just the same.
Having a bond between mother and daughter
Is more than just giving her your name.

God put you in my life
Because He knew you needed me.
Now I know it was in His plan
That as your mother I needed to be.

I love you so much, my little one
Everything you do touches my heart.
I count the minutes, hours and days
While we have to be apart.

I know Mother's Day is for Mamas
But in a way they are for daughters, too.
There is one thing I know, my darling Kira,
I couldn't be a happy mother if I didn't have you.

DAY #172   MY HEART BROKE DOWN AND CRIED

Daily Blessing – *II Corinthians 12:9 "And He said unto me, My grace is sufficient for thee: for my strength is made perfect in weakness. Most gladly therefore will I rather glory in my infirmities, that the power of Christ may rest upon me."*

Sondra and I were talking last night about her brother's death and her mother's illness. She made a comment and the more I thought about it the more this poem came to mind. She asked me if I'd ever been so sad that my heart just broke down and cried.

MY HEART BROKE DOWN AND CRIED

There are times I've hurt so deep within,
But had to keep a smile outside.
Even though there wasn't a tear around,
My heart broke down and cried.

There are times the pain's so great,
The hurt so deep inside.
But I couldn't let the whole world know
So my heart broke down and cried.

I lost a loved one who was my best friend
To hold the emotion within I tried.
Even though the tears flowed freely,
No one could see that my heart cried.

They say that emotion
Does not come from the heart.
Then why sometimes when the world closes in,
It feels like it's coming a part?

So if you see me smiling,
I may be taking life in stride,
When deep down inside I'm hurting,
'Cause my heart broke down and cried.

One of the things that made my heart break down and cry was thinking about how much I missed my grandson. I did have Christopher on my mind a lot today. I didn't know if I'd ever be able to tell him just how much I missed him and wanted to be with him during this time so I decided to put my thoughts to paper so he'd possibly understand in later years.

TO MY GRANDSON, CHRISTOPHER

Oh my darling grandson, Christopher,
My precious little boy.
You'll never really know
How you've filled my life with joy.

From the moment that I held you
In my loving arms,
I was bound and determined
To keep you from life's harms.

There are so many things
That I need to share from my heart
And even though you can't understand

I don't think it's too early to start.
Soon you'll take your first steps
And I won't need to carry you anymore.
But carrying you was always a pleasure
It was never any chore.

And soon those tiny steps,
Will soon lead you away.
But there is so much to teach you
Before that fateful day.

The hardest things to teach you
Are the values you will need.
But, Christopher, believe me when I say
These values you must always heed.

Honesty is the first one,
A trait high above them all.
For if you are honest, little man,
You can always stand tall.

Integrity is the next.
Always be good as your word.
Then every time you speak
You won't worry if you're heard.

Keep a loving spirit
For your fellow man.
And always be there
To lend a helping hand.

But most important, my little one
Is to God always be true.
Keep your eye upon Him
And He will keep His eyes on you.

DAY #173   A LITTLE CLOUD CRIED

I was looking out of the little three-inch window beside my bunk and I saw the plants and flowers that looked so parched. Just then we had a small rain shower and they quickly perked up. I thought how much our lives are like that. When things seem dark and barren, God pours His love down and picks us up.

A LITTLE CLOUD CRIED

A little flower was wilting
To lift its leaves it tried.
Then God saw the flower
And a little cloud cried.

A fish was trying to swim
In a creek almost dried.
Then God saw the fish
And a big cloud cried.

A field of wheat was parched
The stalks brittle and fried.
Then God saw the field
And the whole sky cried.

My life was lost and barren,
No matter what I tried.
But God smiled down and sent His Son
And all of Heaven cried.

This turned out to be one of the favorite of all the poems requested by others.

DAY #174   THE VISITOR

I had been privileged to have several conversations that day about how drugs had moved in and taken over their lives. There had not been a single female that came through those doors that told me that they set out to become a drug addict. Every one of them thought it was something they could handle but it got out of control so quickly. The Lord put this on my heart so that possibly others would understand.

There is a line in this poem that is similar to the one that I used in my poem to Catherine. I didn't realize it until after I finished it. It is so ironic how differently the meanings and consequences of the line, "I got it from you," can have when referring to the example we set. *What is perceived by our children can so easily be either a positive influence or destructive to the point of death.*

THE VISITOR

There is a visitor in our house
Who's taken up residence here.
And even though I use to like him
Now he fills me with fear.

The times I would visit him
Use to be too seldom to speak.
But then it became more often
Even four or five times a week.

Then one day I brought him home,
Just for convenience sake.
How was I to know in the end
It would be my biggest mistake.

The more he hung around
The more impact he had on me.
Even my family and friends noticed
But I had become too blind to see.

I screamed at my kids.
I let the household go.
He was so much fun at the start
How was I to know?

Then one day I saw the signs
He'd been visiting my daughter, too.
And when I tried to punish her, she said
"But, Mama, I got him from you."

Now here I sit
In an emergency room chair.
Because of his last visit with my daughter
Once again, he's brought us despair.

He wrecked our lives
And cause us so much pain.
Don't ever let this visitor in
By the way, his name is cocaine.

DAY #175 **CALLING ON GOD**

Daily Blessing – *Philippians 4:6 "Be careful for nothing; but in every thing by prayer and supplication with thanksgiving let your requests be made known unto God."*

I have gotten so tired of hearing God's name taken in vain and then they issue a plea for Him to get them out of here The Lord wouldn't let me rest tonight until I put these words on paper.

CALLING ON GOD

"Lord, get me out of this place,"
Is a phrase I hear all the time.
But were you thinking about the Lord
When you committed your crime?

When you stuck that needle in your arm
The "Oh, God" you cried out
Was it meant for God to stop you?
Or just something for you to shout?

When you pulled that trigger,
And watched the blood flow free,
The "Jesus" that you uttered,
Was if for your victim you made that plea?

Or when you took a hit on that pipe
Or snorted that powder up your nose,
Were you thinking about God's high?
Or just trying to forget your lows?

Every time we call on Him
He listens to what we have to say.
And if His name is spoken in vain,
He starts turning a deaf ear our way.

So, don't call on Him
Unless it's from the heart.
God may be the finisher of things,
But He'd rather be there from the start.

DAY #176   PRE-SENTENCE INVESTIGATION

Fifty-six days ago I was promised by the court that it would take no more than sixty days for my PSI to come back and then I could go home. What the attorney failed to tell me was that was 60 days from the time I filled out the PSI form. That day came today. I was sent to the front office to be interviewed by a parole officer from Monroe who had been assigned to take my information.

He asked me every question you could imagine, including my family, my education, where I had lived and quite a few questions that you never would ever think of, but at least the process was beginning. Another sixty days, but there is light at the end of the tunnel. I'm afraid the way things have been going that the light is only the train coming to run over me once again.

DAY #177   STARTED LAUNDRY JOB

There were only two jobs in the whole prison that could be held by a pre-trial inmate and that was one of the two laundry jobs; day laundry and night laundry. The night laundry job included uniforms and towels and was done by Brenda.

The day laundry schedule varied each day of the week. Mondays was underwear in the laundry bags (tied properly so they wouldn't open), pajamas and t-shirts but you could only have 2 loads per dorm. Tuesdays were sheets each week and blankets every other week. Wednesdays were the same as Mondays except you could put your sweats in. Thursday was commissary and there was no laundry. Friday was the same as Monday.

Each day the clothes were put in a large laundry buggy, wheeled down to the laundry room, sorted, washed, dried and put back on the cart, and wheeled back into the dorm. It took anywhere from four to five hours to do the laundry because there were four other dorms and only three working washers and dryers. No one could leave the laundry area until all of the dorms were finished.

The worst part of the job was that you had to give up your morning naptime. Doris had done this job until she went home and then Holly took it over. Holly wanted to give it up and asked me if I would take it. Why in the world would I want to do it?

One simple reason, it got me out of the dorm.

DAY #178   GOD'S LITTLE REWARDS

There was another perk to the laundry job. It put me right outside of E dorm where my friend Valerie was now assigned, because she was a kitchen worker. I actually got to have short conversations with her and it was so refreshing. God knew I needed that shot in the arm and I thank Him for it.

I know He had a hand in it because one way I always judged how good my poems were, was through the amount of tears that I saw Valerie cry when she read them. This was a "treat" I hadn't been able to witness in quite a while. Even though we weren't allowed to have direct correspondence, I had a friend on the outside that I'd send copies of my poems and she would forwarded them back to Valerie.

About a week before I took the laundry job, I sent Elaine a poem for Valerie to give to her mother. The first morning of my laundry job, I saw Valerie open the letter from Elaine and read that poem. I truly didn't think I'd get to see that again. God knew I needed that shot in the arm and I thanked Him for it!

The Lord allowed me to see through that experience, that tears can be beautiful when they are shed for the right reasons.

TO SEE YOU CRY

My friend, to see you cry
Can bring me heartache and grief.
When those tears are the only thing
That gives you any relief.

My friend, to see you cry,
Can put a smile in my heart
Because your joyous tears of emotion
I am privileged to be a part.

The tears that always break my heart
Are those I've caused by hurting you.
'Cause believe me, dear friend,
That's the last thing I'd ever want to do.

But the tears you shed, my friend,
That warms me through and through,
Are the ones that are caused by something
I've done that truly touches you.

DAY #180   THE HOLY SPIRIT'S CALMING EFFECT

Because of the constant close proximity to each other, our lives brush up against the lives of others; a wrong word, a rash action, are as much a part of our day in here as eating and sleeping. We are all guilty of them. We all receive them. There is no surprise when they come. Sometimes they issue a challenge for a volley of spiteful comments that only escalate into a physical fight.

Tonight after supper there were several inmates that had been arguing all day and it finally festered into not one fight but three or four.

Ms. Carter, the supervisor, had enough and knew the only way to control the situation was to send us all to our bunks. The tension was so thick that you could actually feel it in the air. Even though everyone was confined to their small space there was still short quips now directed at the guards instead of each other.

Before I realized it, the Lord had caused me to open my mouth and this is what came out: "Ladies, there is only one Person that can resolve all of these conflicts and bring peace and harmony to us. I think we need to go to God in prayer and ask for His presence, right now."

All I asked was for God to come among us and bring His peace into this turmoil. No sooner had I gotten out, Amen, when Gina started singing from her bunk, *"There's a sweet, sweet spirit in this place, and I know that it's the presence of the Lord."*

When she finished singing Jasmine came out with one of the most beautiful versions of, "The King is Coming," that I've ever heard. Then one by one others started singing and within seconds the air that had been filled with discourse and tension was now filled with the presence of the Holy Spirit.

Those that didn't sing gave their testimonies or read scriptures. As the testimonies wound down, Jasmine started singing, "Amazing Grace." It didn't take long for the whole dorm to join in.

Ms. Grant and Ms. Carter were so touched by the change that had occurred in those 75 women that they dropped all of the restrictions and allowed us to return to our normal activities.

We all knew as the last line of the song so aptly states: *"Without a doubt we'll know that we have been revived when we shall leave this place."*

SOMETIMES HE CALMS THE RAGING STORM

Sometimes He calms the raging storm
Sometimes He just calms me.
Especially when the storms of life
Are something only He can see.

Just like He calmed the storm
Upon the apostles tempest sea.
As their boat was rocked to and fro
He and He alone calms the storms within me.

If anger builds up inside
To the point my temper flares
He lets me now I'm not alone
For He is always there.

When frustrations of the day
Turns my world upside down
He lovingly tells my inner spirit
How to turn it back around.

When someone has hurt my feelings
And the tears weld up deep inside.
He reaches down and dries each one
Reassuring me within His love I'll always abide.

So, let the storms of life come my way
Because He keeps me right where I need to be.
Thank God sometimes He calms the storms themselves
And sometimes He just calms me.

My evening prayer – *"Thank you, Father, for your calming and reviving Spirit that is ever present with us. Help us understand that all we have to do is ask and you'll calm the raging storms around us, whether they be problems, situations or even people."*

DAY #181   AN INMATE'S FAMILY

With today being Mother's Day, my thoughts turn to family. Family is the center point of most of our lives. When we're happy, sad, afraid or in need of comfort, it is most often our family that we turn to. Many of the problems of today can be attributed to the disintegration of the family unit.

The family of an inmate, whether guilty or not guilty, suffers right along side the inmate as though they were as guilty as the inmate. They wait and worry and are often humiliated at the hands of the prison officials who they are forced to deal with. Many times they are shunned by society because most of the public erroneously thinks that if you are arrested, you must be guilty. The only guilt these family members face is the guilt that they place on themselves in feeling that they have failed their inmate in some form or fashion.

DAY #182   WITNESSING FOR ELIZABETH

I was still working on Elizabeth; unfortunately her mother and the devil seemed to be winning. Other girls in the dorm were still giving her a hard time and shunning her for the least little thing. God made me see that sometimes it's not what we say or preach, but how we use our lives as a testimony to Him. As a good friend of mine used to say "What you do speaks so loud that I can't hear what you say."

OUR LIFE IS A TESTIMONY

Job was a man of God
Who loved and served the Lord.
Because of his faithfulness,
By God he was adored.

But God told Satan:
"Tempt my man Job and you will see"
"You can take away all he owns"
"But he'll never let you have his testimony."

Satan did just as he was challenged,
There wasn't any persecution he didn't try.
Job's friends were even telling him,
"Just curse God and die."

Job stood strong and lived for God.
His testimony to others stood true.
If God would let Satan tempt a man like Job
Nothing will stop Satan from trying me and you.

Our life is a testimony
That we live everyday.
We must use it to glorify God
In each and every way.

Your soul is only one resident
That through God's mercy Satan lost to hell.
But how many souls has old Lucifer gained
By others watching your testimony as it fell.

If you can't show the lost
Christ like qualities so true
Why should they want Jesus in their lives
I sure would wonder, wouldn't you?

So be careful and look around
When Satan starts tempting you.
Be careful how and what you choose
For you never know just who's watching you.

I found out that a good friend of Elizabeth was dying from a injuries he'd received in a fight. When I saw how upset she was and knew she had no belief in God, I wondered who did she and others that aren't founded in faith, turn to at times like this.

WHO DO YOU TURN TO?

Who do you turn to
In your time of grief?
Without knowing God
Where do you go for relief?

Who do you go to,
When your world has fallen apart?
Only God, and God alone
Can soothe a broken heart.

You think the Bible's just a story book
Full of fables and tales.
Then how come throughout all times
God's word never fails?

Even if there is no heaven or hell after death
One thing is perfectly clear.
It's good to have the Lord on your side
Everyday you're alive and here.

I'll pray for your, my friend
That God will show you the way.
'Cause I want our friendship to continue
Long after Judgment Day.

DAY #183   IT COULD HAPPEN TO YOU

I realized that it had been exactly six months to the day since I had spoken with my mother or any other member of my family, save my children. I knew I was being judged by each of them without benefit of hearing my side of the story. I knew that when I got out I'd be shunned if not totally disowned by them, but I had gained so much that it didn't really matter any longer. I was allowed to see them for what they really were and, how all of the years I obsessed with trying to please them was in vain.

It took all of this to make me appreciate the fact that the only family member I needed to please was the One who didn't judge me or desert me, but reassured me just how much He loved me. I wrote this to let them and others know just how easy the same thing could happen to any one of them.

IT COULD HAPPEN TO YOU

I am a convicted felon
A label I'll carry all my life.
Even though I may not be guilty
It will cause a certain amount of strife.

And even if I were guilty
My debt to society is paid.
So why are there those who won't let it rest
For one mistake I might have made.

So, now I'm in the free world,
My lessons have been learned.
My freedom from my past mistakes,
Surely is something I have learned.

I'm sure there's been times
When you've done something not right.
The only difference between you and me
Was your crime was not brought to light.

Don't judge me for my record
When we meet don't look the other way,
For all you know without warning,
It could happen to you one day.

DAY #188   NATALIE

This poem was inspired by Natalie. Natalie was a girl in her late teens. She had married young and had a son right away. I don't know if she knew it prior to the marriage or if she found out afterwards that her husband was abusive. Either way her son suffered a broken hip and a dislocated arm while she was at work. It was at the hands of her husband. What made it bad for her was she didn't report it nor seek medical treatment for the 2 month old until several days later.

Over the last few months I watched Natalie grow and mature. She had to watch her son, Kyle, grow through pictures. Natalie's family lived in Florida but they did make several trips to see her and the baby. The courts felt the child was better off with foster parents than with Natalie's parents.

She came to me tonight and told me that the next morning she would go into court and have her parental rights terminated so that another couple could adopt her young son. She cried as she told me it was the hardest decision she'd ever made but she had to admit that she had a lot more growing to do before she could resume her role as a mother. She didn't want Kyle to suffer for her mistakes any more than he already had.

The foster parents that wanted to adopt the baby were good about sending pictures and keeping her updated on Kyle. It was easy to tell by the pictures and letters that they sent that they loved that little boy very much and he was incredibly happy. They promised she could have contact with Kyle when she finished serving her time.

She wanted me to write a poem that she could put up for him to read in years to come that might help him understand why she did what she did by giving him two loving parents that would make sure no harm would ever come to him, again. This is what the Lord put on my heart.

MY DEAREST DARLING CHILD

My dearest darling child
There's something I need you to know
It's something I've been wanting to tell you
Since a very long time ago.

Now that you're a young adult
I hope these things you'll understand.
Those words are from your Mother's heart
Not just writings from her hand.

Before you were born, my precious dear,
I made some decisions that were wrong.
And no matter what you're told or think,
Mama loved you all along.

Those decisions caused me to be separated
From the little one I loved so dear.
But without this time apart for Mama to grow
What would've happened I could only fear.

But I made sure in my absence
That you were loved and well cared for.
You had a host around you
That couldn't have loved you any more.

But the two greatest things I left with you
Was, of course, my undying love,
And a special guardian angel to protect you
God sent down from Heaven up above.

So always remember, my little one,
How much Mama loves you so.
The proof of my love was not in the staying
It was in my choosing to go.

DAY #195   THE SPARROW

Daily Blessing – *Matthew 6:26 "Behold the fowls of the air; for they sow not, neither do they reap, nor gather into barns; yet your Heavenly Father feedeth them. Are ye not much better than they?"*

After I read this passage, I walked to the back of the dorm. There by the back door was one of the few windows we were privileged to have. The window only measured three inches wide and about six feet tall but it allowed a good view of the small recreation yard behind our dorm. This area was surrounded by a ten-foot cyclone fence crowned with barbed wire and coiled ribbons of razor wire.

I watched a small sparrow as he flitted from the wire to the ground and back again. Never once did he land on the sharp barbs of either wire. He always managed to land safe and secure

But of course he would, because he listened to God's guidance and direction without question or debate. How much better our lives would be if we did the same.

THE SPARROW

As I looked out my prison window
On a yard of fence and locks
I saw a sparrow frolicking
Without a worry of schedules or clocks.

As I watched him scurry about
From ground to razor wire coiled
I wondered how he knew where to land
So as not even one feather to spoil.

Then I remembered that old spiritual
That Ethel Waters sang
God's eye is truly on the sparrow
But the thought caused my heart a pang.

It made me realize the times God spoke to me
But His instructions I did not heed.
My life wound up on the razor's sharp
Because I would not let Him take the lead.

If we would open our hearts to God
And let Him guide the way
We'd be as carefree as that sparrow
As we go through life each day.

Too many times we just pray to God
And tell Him what to do.
But how often do you just meditate
And wait for God to talk to you.

The next time on life's highway
When you contemplate an uncertain turn
Remember that sparrow on the wire
And for God's guidance you'll soon yearn.

DAY #199   EMOTIONAL GAMES

Survival is perfected to an art in prison. One of the greatest arts that must be learned is "game playing." I'm not talking about board games or card games but head games; some safe, some not so safe.

The most dangerous head game I've found involves people's emotions. In pre-trial, "bulldagging" is just fly-by-night. Every one knows the rules and no one get hurts.

In the DOC dorms where there is a little more permanence, it becomes the "art of the chase." Prison can and is a very lonely place where one of the basic human instincts, "the need for intimacy and belonging" is sought after in many ways. Since I am speaking of women whose sentences range anywhere from a couple of months to those that probably will never see the free world again, some relationships become very volatile.

I sit back and watch as people's emotions are played with like yoyos. It could be based on commissary or just the rush received from the power of "winning" someone's affection. Unfortunately, I've seen many who didn't know the rules get hurt.

You have to realize that most of these women suffer from low self-esteem and crave even the slightest bit of attention. This gives those that would take advantage of this situation an enormous amount of power to control "their victim," like a puppet. Regrettably, this puppet has a heart and this heart gets broken when the perpetrator moves on to the next tender, young target.

Then there are those who know the game plan and flit from one to another with about as much emotion as a honey bee has for the flower whose nectar it robs. It appears as if they are hurting so much that the only way to relieve their pain is to spread it around to others. Thus, "playing the game" momentarily feeds their self-esteem or more precisely, their ego.

Game playing is so important that it has a vernacular all its own. Some of the most common phrases are, "Can't play no G with me," and. "Don't hate the player, hate the game."

Day #204   Broken Glasses

I sat down on my bunk and forgot that I had placed my glasses on the mattress. Needless to say the butt proved to be heavier than the earpiece and it broke. God even had a plan in this. I was allowed to go down to medical and glue the broken earpiece. Because pill call was such a busy time, making sure all the inmates took their medicine and didn't sneak it back to the dorm to sell; I had to go down late that night. Miss Adele was on as nurse and I got to have a very pleasant and uplifting visit with her as the glue dried. It gave me a whole new viewpoint and respect for the ladies that dedicated their lives to guard and protect us.

TO THE OFFICERS OF RPDC

To the officers of Richland Parish Detention Center
My hat goes off to you.
For few have the commitment
To do the job you chose to do.

Everyday you come to work,
You are face with ridicule and scorn.
Because it is your job to protect and maintain
Those whose lives are bitter and forlorn.

There are a lot of thankless ones
Who curse and disrespect you to your face.
They seem to lack the knowledge
You didn't put them in this place.

You have to have the skills of a nurse
To handle drunks and those with DT's, too.
You have to have the wisdom of a counselor
To the lost souls that confide in you.

You have to have the patience of Job
For those that try you like a child.
Sometimes you must posses the strength of Sampson
For the occasional ones that go wild.

You have to be a peacemaker
When things get out of hand,
And put situations on rational terms,
For those who do not understand.

But let me say during my time here,
You've treated me with nothing but respect.
I've seen you go the extra mile
You always gave more than you'd ever get.

So once again, I salute you
For all you've done for me.
You've made my stay as pleasant as possible,
For someplace I didn't want to be.

So take pride in a job well done
Although I really suspect.
The job is more of a commitment,
That deserves a lot of respect.

DAY #205   THE LIGHT INSIDE

So many have come through those doors that have made drugs their master for so long it didn't take a trained expert to tell exactly what plagued them.   The old trite statement that the eyes are the window to your soul is so appropriate.   When I looked into most of their eyes it was like looking in a deep, dark, empty hole.

THE LIGHT INSIDE

I look at your face
And see what you've become.
And I silently wish
The damage could be undone.

Eyes that once must have sparkled
Now have gone cold and dead.
The love that once shone through them
Is replaced with emptiness and dread.

Skin that once must have been silky
Like a mornings first dew,
Now is weathered and scarred
From the abuse you've put yourself through.

But all of that's on the outside
The worst damage I fear is within,
From all the ways you used to escape
The pain of what might have been.

The light in your heart
That shines through your whole being.
Has been snuffed out by abuse
And the real you it keeps us from seeing.

It's not too late to re-ignite that spark.
By letting the love of God in your heart.
It won't undo all the years of damage
But it's the best way to start.

I quit my laundry job today so that Glenda could get the picnic visit privilege. Her son was being shipped to Iraq within a couple of months and I felt that she would enjoy spending the time with him.

DAY #206   STORMS OUTSIDE

There was a very bad storm last night.   The rain on the tin roof only intensified the feeling of the imminent danger we all felt. The Lord moved me to make mention that we were in God's Hands because there was a lot of uneasiness throughout the dorm. This morning while lining up for breakfast, one of the inmates commented that my remark had brought her comfort and allowed her to sleep a lot better.

DAY #212   RUMORS OF BSCF

The long awaited transfer to the new penal farm at Plain Dealing was anxiously anticipated by a lot of the pre-trial inmates from Bossier Parish. I was not included in that lot. Fortunately or unfortunately as the case may be, I've always believed the devil you know is better than the one you don't know. The biggest drawback to the new facility is that it is a non-smoking facility. Maybe this is the hesitancy I feel but if it is meant by God for me to go there, then He'll give me the strength to survive. Whether it's here or there I pray my time is not much longer. I'll take whatever time remaining the same as I've done the last seven months, one day at a time. I look to God for the purpose He has in my staying that day.

DAY #213   I'M IN YOUR HANDS, GOD

Daily Blessing – *John 15:16 "Ye have not chosen Me, but I have chosen you, and ordained you, that ye should go and bring forth fruit, and that your fruit should remain: that whatsoever ye shall ask of the Father in My name, He may give it you."*

I've had a strange feeling all day. It may be the ultra sweet cinnamon roll and coffee for breakfast, commissary with Pepsi and 2 more cups of coffee, a package of cookies topped off with a double chocolate cookie stuffed with marshmallow cream for supper that has me feeling a little anxious.

It could be the full moon approaching or just maybe it's the rumors that are flying about us being moved to Plain Dealing. It's more a feeling of sadness than anxiety. The latest rumor is we'll be leaving Monday after lunch. If I don't get to court Monday, I guess I'll see for myself. I've finally made my peace with the move. The hardest part will be not smoking, but it shouldn't be for long. My impending freedom is just around the corner. God has a purpose in everything He does.

That's why I pray every night, "Not my will, but God's will be done." He's brought me through this far. As the bible says in John 14:1, *"Let not your heart be troubled..."*

So, as always, God, I'm in Your hands. I found it's the safest place to be.

DAY #214   THE PASSION OF CHRIST

Daily Blessing – Romans 5:8 *"But God commendeth His love toward us, in that, while we were yet sinners, Christ died for us."*

Today some of us had the unique opportunity of not just watching a movie on the passion of Christ but also to experience it and what He actually went through for each and everyone of us. I Peter 2:24 says that *"by His stripes we are healed."* That means that every time that rod was slapped across His back and every time that whip cut through His flesh, it was for me.

I noticed a great many tears on a great many faces and I felt the need to take that movie one step farther..

After the prayer that night, I added the following invitation:

"If any of you felt a strange feeling within your heart while watching The Passion of Christ today and you are not sure what it might have been, it is very possible God is speaking to you to make a decision for Him.

"Christ took the hard part, so our part could be easy. All you have to do is say a very simple prayer admitting to God that you are a sinner, that you are truly sorry for all of the sins you have committed and that you accept Jesus as your Lord and Savior."

That's all it takes to bring Jesus that twelve inches from your head to your heart and to Him it will make all the pain and suffering He endured, worth it."

CHRIST DIED FOR ME!

I never really gave much thought
To what Christ had done just for me.
Until a dream I had one night
And through it what God allowed me to see.

I was standing in the crowd
When Jesus was brought to them.
I could feel the disappointment He felt
As they all cried "Crucify Him!"

I followed the procession
As it led up Calvary's hill.
And watched as Christ faced the anguish
For what He knew to be God's will.

The stripes that cut into His back
Each time the whip was cracked
Were placed there because of me
And the faith that I had lacked.

And on the way to Calvary
I saw how many times He stumbled and fell.
Because of the heavy cross He carried
So I wouldn't have to face the anguish of hell.

I stood and watched in horror
As they laid Him on the tree.
That's when I knew in my heart
He was facing all this because of me.

My stubborn pride that excluded
Christ from my daily plans,
Provided the force that sent the nails
All the way through His hands.

With each blow of the hammer
That drove the nails through His feet,
I saw each time I ran from God
Only for my sins to repeat.

The stabbing crown of thorns
Pressed down in His head
Was woven very carefully
Of every malicious word I had ever said.

The sharpness of my tongue
Each and every time I lied
Was transferred to the sword
As it was thrust through His side.

I saw His final moments
As His life started to dim.
Because of my life long rejection
I witnessed His Own Father forsake Him.

When I awoke I suddenly knew
What Christ wanted me to see:
That He would have rather died
Than to live eternally without me.

PART III
50 DAYS IN THE WILDERNESS

DAY # 219   INTO THE WILDERNESS

Daily Blessing – *Job 1:3 "Every place that the sole of your foot shall tread upon, that have I given unto you, as I said unto Moses."*

This was the day that some of the inmates had been waiting for in anticipation and others were dreading. We were being transferred to Bossier Sheriff's Correctional Facility in Plain Dealing.

The prison dress in prisons reflects the old idea that in order to make bad people good it is necessary to make them as uncomfortable and ugly as possible.

Undoubtedly Bossier Sheriff's Correctional Facility held to this concept. What could be more humiliating than red and white striped uniforms?

Eight of us were forced to spend hours in small holding cells while all of the others were being processed. Finally, it was my turn.

The desk guard went through every item in my sack, discarding most of the things I had accumulated at Rayville. We were not allowed personal sheets, personal blankets, nor any articles of clothing that wasn't white. Any food items that were opened, such as my coffee, was discarded.

Once again I was starting from scratch but this time there would be no packages. They weren't allowed. Everything we would acquire had to be bought on commissary at inflated prices but I wouldn't be buying cigarettes, BSCF was a non-smoking facility. That left a few dollars more for hygiene items and snacks!

After we were processed we were put in the dorm. Toward the front of the room were six metal tables with benches built on them. That is where we were to eat. Our food would be brought to us, no cafeteria. With a maximum of ten people per table that would mean only sixty people could sit and eat at once. The dorm held seventy-five inmates. No leaving the dorm. Great planning!

The dorm had seventy-five beds, just like Rayville, but the bunks around the walls were not double bunks, but triple bunks. To keep the top bunk from being too far off the ground, the distance between each of the layers was shortened, considerably. If you were unfortunate enough to be on one of the bottom two layers, you found it was totally impossible to sit up in your bed without crouching over in a most uncomfortable position.

It was a brand new jail, clean and pristine but cold both in temperature and temperament. The guards demanded that they be addressed as Officer and their last name. At Rayville it was Ms. Kathy or Ms. Jesse, Ms. Parnell, etc. The guards at BSCF took great pride in bragging that they were deputies, allowed to carry guns, as opposed to the "rent-a-cops" (as they referred to them) at Rayville. RPDC was a privately owned facility and the guards were paid by a private corporation instead of being deputies.

One of the most humiliating experiences of the day was when one of the guards, Deputy Lynn, came in and to get our attention and actually said, '1-2-3, all eyes on me."

I could tell that the time I was to spend in this place was going to be an experience, but I knew it wasn't anything the Lord and I couldn't handle.

DAY # 222   THE BATTLE IS NOT OURS

Daily Blessing - *II Chronicles 20:15 "And he said, Hearken ye, all Judah, and ye inhabitants of Jerusalem, and thou king Jehoshaphat, Thus saith the LORD unto you, Be not afraid nor dismayed by reason of this great multitude; for the battle is not yours, but God's."*

Oh God, when does this storm end? I sit here tonight trying to figure out the lessons you want me to learn.

Why is it that when things are tough it takes all of my energy just to get through the day? I know I have been praying to you every day but somehow by putting my words to You on paper seems to make things more real.. So much has happened and I don't know where to begin.

You more than anyone know my heart and my mind. You know the pain I have felt over the betrayal of my mother and brother, but You've shown me that You, as my Father, will never leave or betray me.

You've allowed me to lose everything, but used that loss to show me that through You, I've gained the world.

You've shown me just how treacherous those that profess to be friends can be, but You've put wonderful trusted friends in my path.

Your love and power continues to amaze me. I am so grateful, God, to have personally witnessed how Your love will always overcome evil, each and every time.

DAY # 228   BELIEVE IN YOURSELF

This poem is about the three principles God showed me that I needed to pass along to the younger inmates; so many of them suffer from low self-esteem.

Most of them have been told all of their lives that they count for nothing; they can't do anything and will never amount to anything. This added to the abuses they have faced, whether emotional or physical, only compound the low self worth.

I added these three principles to the end of the prayer each night and it seemed to help some of the younger girls, as well as a few of the older ones.

BELIEVE IN YOURSELF

God believes in you.
He did two of the greatest things He could do.
He created you in His own image
And sent His Son to die for you.

I believe in you
For I see the you that can be
All you need is to ask God to bring it out
For the entire world to see.

Now start believing in yourself
And all the possibilities God's opened for you.
With a little faith in God and yourself
There's nothing the two of you can't do.

DAY # 233   COURT DATE SET

Daily Blessing – *Romans 12:12 "Rejoicing in hope; patient in tribulation; continuing instant in prayer."*

Today was a day for rejoicing. I finally got the letter I'd been waiting for, for so long. It was from the Bossier Parish District Attorney's office informing me that I had a July 14th court date.

Hopefully this meant I would be going home in fourteen days. I pray there is nothing that can go wrong, now.

DAY # 234   WHEN NIGHT TIME FALLS

Sondra wrote to Jeanette and asked her to have me a note to write a poem with the title, "When Nighttime Falls." This is what the Lord put on my heart.

WHEN NIGHTTIME FALLS

During the waking hours
This place is a beehive all around
For where there is noise and confusion
It covers your pain with sound.

You make it through the day
The best way you know how.
You're living for a future date
Trying hard not to think about now.

But when nighttime falls
Upon this dreary place,
The lights go out above us
Each one retreats into their own space.

There they lay and dream
Of a time that's not quite here,
When they'll walk into freedom
And everyone will cheer.

They dream of the children
Someone else is having to keep,
All because of lustful pleasures,
Mama's not there to watch them sleep.

But most of all they just dream
For the darkness is easier to take.
The dream become their reality.
The nightmare is only when they awake.

DAY # 235   BULLDAGGING

Eight of the girls were pulled out of the dorm tonight and sent to Sergeant Maggio, the nighttime supervisor. It seems that there were cameras hidden in the dorm that none of us knew about. They were caught in the one activity that is illegal in any prison, bulldagging. This activity isn't banned because of any moral reasons because most guards don't really care about morality. What does concern them are the arguments and fights that break out because of one inmate's claim on another. This is usually challenged by a more aggressive inmate. But this is a very good explanation for homosexual activities in prison, be it male or female.

I can relate to a true homosexual relationship better than most. This is another example of how God uses people and events in our lives to prepare us for upcoming situations. For over 20 years I lived in a gay relationship.

With God there are no accidents, no coincidences. This is true for the events in our lives as well as the people we meet and those with whom we develop friendships and relationships. Many times He purposefully plants these friends on our path to aid us in physical, emotional and spiritual growth. How we cultivate these friendships is entirely up to us.

For more than 20 years I had a very dear friend, whom I can say, unequivocally, God sent me to get through my divorce and help raise my girls while providing me with the emotional support He knew I so desperately needed. It was my sinful, lustful desires and actions that turned that precious friendship into a relationship unacceptable in the eyes of God. Whereas, I made my peace with God over the homosexual aspect of that relationship, I still thank Him for the lessons Mimi taught me about life, myself and loving others. As I have heard so many times in so many different ways, Gods hates the sin but loves the sinner. As God promises all of us in Psalms 103:12 *"As far as the east is from the west, so far hath He removed our transgressions from us;' I know I am forgiven."*

"Bulldagging" is unlike homosexual relationships that are formed in the outside world, but my own experience did allow me a greater insight and understanding. Rather than form gangs in prison, women tend to create pseudo families in which they adopt various family roles– father, mother, daughter, sister – in a type of half serious, half play-acting set of relationships. Some of these roles, but not all of them, involve homosexual relationships.

In jail the word lesbian seldom, if ever, is mentioned. The absence of sexual consummation is only partially explained by prison prohibition against any kind of sexual behavior. Basically the women are not looking for sex. They are looking for love, for concern and companionship, for relief from the overwhelming sense of isolation and solitude that pervades each of us.

Once in prison changes in roles are common. Many women who are strictly heterosexual in the street become "butch" in prison. "Fems" often create butches by convincing an inmate that she would make a "cute butch." *About 80 percent of the prison population engage in some form of homosexual relationship. Almost all follow negative, stereotypic male/ female role models.*

Women who are "aggressive" or who play the masculine roles are referred to as butches, bulldaggers or stud broads. They are always in demand because they are always in the minority. Women who are "passive," or who play feminine roles are referred to as fems. The butch-fem relationships are often oppressive, resembling the most oppressive, exploitative aspect of a sexist society. It is typical to hear butches threatening fems with physical violence and it is not uncommon for butches to actually beat their "women." Some butches consider themselves pimps and go with the women who have the most commissary, the most contraband or the best outside connections. They feel that they are a class above ordinary women, which entitles them to "respect." A butch will usually refer to another butch as, "man."

And often the lesbian relationships that occur are very abusive. The role that one of the women will play will be an exaggerated male role reproducing everything that you might see in a heterosexual relationship.

DAY # 237   TRUE FREEDOM

Dear Mama,

You can't really appreciate celebrating freedom until you no longer have it to celebrate. Since my last holiday, a bunch of us have been transferred to a new prison in Plain Dealing. Bossier Parish no longer pays RPDC to house those that are awaiting trial so we must be the guinea pigs and try out the new facility.

At RPDC we did have a little more freedom and privilege than we are allowed here. Most of our personal belongings that we were allowed at RPDC have been taken away from us. We no longer go to a chow hall but our meals are brought in to us.

It has been almost 2 months and we have not been allowed to leave these four walls that contain us. Sometimes we wonder if there is even an outside left because there is no windows except for a very small slit where the ceiling meets the top of the concrete wall about 20 feet high.

The one thing I miss the most is the ability to go to church occasionally. Here there are no church services and I see so many wandering away from the Lord because of the lack of the spiritual guidance we had at RPDC.

All this loss of the freedom I felt on the outside and the few freedoms I had at RPDC has made me more mindful that no matter what man may do there is one freedom that can't be taken away. That is the freedom that was given to me by my Heavenly Father when I accepted Christ as my Lord and Savior. Romans 8:2 "For the law of the Spirit of life in Christ Jesus hath made me free from the law of sin and death." This is the only true freedom that exists.

It is ironic that with this holiday for celebrating freedom I have finally learned when my imprisonment will finally come to an end. I hope to have a little less than a year before I can return home. That means that next July the 4th, I will celebrate the freedom not only given to me by men but most importantly the freedom given me by Christ who bought my freedom with a price, His own life.

Love always,
Your daughter, Tracey

TRUE FREEDOM

On this July 4th while other celebrate freedom
I'll be celebrating in jail,
But this year I'm freer now
Than ever before, without fail

Freedom's more than something physical,
It's more a state of mind.
You can be imprisoned while in the free world
Or free behind bars, I find.

I may not be able to leave
Through these locked doors right now,
But my spirit and my heart soar free.
I know you're dying to ask me how.

My freedom comes through Jesus,
My Master and my King,
Who died for my salvation
And freed me from sin to life everlasting.

I may be in prison
For something I did or didn't do.
But Jesus Christ spent time in jail
For something He was innocent of, too.

There are those who seem free as a bird,
But to sin are totally enslaved.
Who always meant to turn to God;
The road to hell with good intentions are paved.

So thank you, Lord, for my freedom,
Freedom that man cannot take away.
Freedom that I will celebrate
From now until Judgment Day.

DAY # 240   WITNESSING TO TIFFANY

Daily Blessing – *Deuteronomy 33:27 "The eternal God is thy refuge, and underneath are the everlasting arms: and He shall thrust out the enemy from before thee; and shall say, Destroy them."*

A bad storm caused Laquisha to become troubled about end times. Laquisha wasn't much over 19 and just a couple of months pregnant. This particular night there was a terrible storm with tornado warnings coming across the television every few minutes.

I had acquired the title of, "Nana," during my stay at RPDC because a lot of the young girls looked to me as a grandmother and would come to me for advice. I had outlasted most of the inmates that were in the dorm when I first arrived, so it made me "an old timer." My grandson had started calling me "Nana" shortly before I was arrested and they just continued the tradition.

Laquisha came over and sat on my bunk and told me she was scared. She said that she was afraid the end of the world was coming. It reminded me of time when I was just a child and Dr. Tatum was preaching on Revelations. I would come home on Sunday nights afraid to go to sleep. My mother would reassure me by telling me something her mother had told you. *"If we believe in Jesus, we have nothing to worry about concerning the end of time because when we close our eyes in death, that will be our end time and we'll go to live with Him. But if the Lord should return before we die, we have nothing to fear because we'll be in His loving arms."*

I used the same words my mother gave to me. Then I asked her if she had ever accepted Christ as her Savior. She admitted that she really had not. We knelt and prayed right beside my bunk. She asked the Lord into her life. Afterwards, she had a peace that could be seen on her face.

Tracey Brown

DAY # 243   FOUND MY BLESSINGS

Daily Blessing – *Luke 15:3-10 "3: And He spake this parable unto them, saying,*
4: What man of you, having an hundred sheep, if he lose one of them, doth not leave the ninety and nine in the wilderness, and go after that which is lost, until he find it?
5: And when he hath found it, he layeth it on his shoulders, rejoicing.
Lu:15:6: And when he cometh home, he calleth together his friends and neighbors, saying unto them, Rejoice with me; for I have found my sheep which was lost.
7: I say unto you, that likewise joy shall be in heaven over one sinner that repenteth, more than over ninety and nine just persons, which need no repentance.
8: Either what woman having ten pieces of silver, if she lose one piece, doth not light a candle, and sweep the house, and seek diligently till she find it?
9: And when she hath found it, she calleth her friends and her neighbors together, saying, rejoice with me; for I have found the piece which I had lost.
10: Likewise, I say unto you, there is joy in the presence of the angels of God over one sinner that repenteth."

Ever since I found my first "blessing" on my mattress in Rayville, I began dating and keeping them. I had two envelopes full when I came to BSCF. In the move they seemed to have gotten lost. I was sick over it and continually looked for them in what few things I had left.

Today I happen to be going through one of the books that Catherine had sent me when I was at Rayville and there they were.

I know now how the woman that found her coin rejoiced, how the shepherd felt when he found his lost sheep and most importantly how God feels when we find Him. So many of these little pieces of paper played an important role in what was to happen on that particular day or a lesson the Lord wanted me to learn or even at times, what I would write.   These are some of the things that will treasure always.

DAY # 244   MARVIN'S ROOM

It is funny how just one little something that is said, without any significance on its own, sets off a whole myriad of thoughts and ideas in your own mind. Sometimes I feel God uses the simplest things to get my attention. I don't always have to be hit over the head with a hammer. Most of my poems have been conceived and inspired by a single line or thought someone else would relay.

I caught a glimpse of a movie that was playing on television today. I definitely want to see it when I get out. It was called "Marvin's Room."

It must have been part of a higher plan that I catch that particular moment of the movie because of something that was said.

I don't know anything about the plot but one character, Dianne Keaton, told Meryl Streep that her life had been lucky to have had so much love in it. Meryl Streep reassured her that she was loved by all those around her. Diane Keaton said that was not why she was lucky, she was lucky *because she was able to love those around her, not just be loved by them.*

That one phrase nearly blew me away! It made me realize that *the strength of our character is not measured by those that love us, but by those we chose to love.*

I have had the wonderful opportunity to have loved so many in my life. I'm not just talking about family because that is pretty much a given.

I'm talking about all of the people that God has chosen to cross my path throughout my life. He has shown me that each one has some quality within them to love. I've had the love and respect of all those wonderful kids from Agape, and God knows I loved each and every one of them, and still do.

Now I'm surrounded with a whole new audience for my attention and affection. No matter how hard I try to separate myself from the people in this place, I can't help but love each and every one for some strange or simple reason, but it expands my love, whatever the reason may be.

This makes me an extremely lucky and blessed person.

DAY # 245   LIBRARY

There were no provisions at BSCF for educational or vocational training. The women, at the expiration of their sentences, will go out not only worn to physical depletion, but also as illiterate and untrained as they entered. I found that about thirty per cent could neither read nor write, and with few exceptions, the others had not finished the grade schools.

At the time I entered, no library facilities were provided for the women. They were entirely without reading matter except for what they could purchase. Because the food problem was so pressing, it was natural that what little money they could secure should go to feed their stomachs and not their minds.

Today, Kim Ferris and I were asked if we would like to start setting up a library. We both jumped at the chance to get out of the dorm and provide a little entertainment for the other inmates.

We were shown into a small room with only four metal tables and boxes of books. The guard told us to separate these donated books into male and female specific books. Undoubtedly, they were going to set up a male and a female library since the facility housed both genders.

Our enthusiasm soon deflated when we saw the types of books that had been donated. Not only were most of these books outdated and worn but very few seemed appropriate for the type of audience that would be perusing their musty pages. The smell of must was so strong that we had to lay the books out to air before we could even try and sort them.

Amongst all of this disorder I found a gem that I'm sure God planted for me to find. It was a small book that looked practically new and even though all of the other books were covered in dust, this one seemed as fresh and new as the day it was purchased. It was a small book like one might send in place of a greeting card. The condition not only caught my eye but the title peaked my interest; *"The Greatest of These Is Love."*

When the guard came to take us back to the dorm, I asked if I might have this book and she willingly complied with my request.

I couldn't wait to get back to my bunk and read through my new found treasure. The book was a sermon preached by Henry Drummond, a Scottish scientist turned preacher. Even though this particular sermon was preached in the late 1800's, its message is still so relevant today. Based on I Corinthians 13, it proves God's message is as true today as it always has been and always will be.

As I read the book, I was reminded of a sermon I heard when I was a young girl. The young preacher was really on fire for the Lord and his sermon on I Corinthians 13 has stuck with me to this very day He taught me the three Greek words for love, philos (brotherly love), Eros (erotic love) and agape (God's type of love). He pointed out that the type of love Paul spoke of in I Corinthians 13 was agape and that is how we are to love one another; the way God loves us, unconditionally.

This book was just a reminder from God for me to go back to that passage because He knew I was going to need it.

I Corinthians 13:1-13, "Though I speak with the tongues of men and of angels, and have not charity (love), I am become as sounding brass, or a tinkling cymbal.
2 And though I have the gift of prophecy, and understand all mysteries, and all knowledge; and though I have all faith, so that I could remove mountains, and have not charity (love), I am nothing.

3 And though I bestow all my goods to feed the poor, and though I give my body to be burned, and have not charity (love), it profiteth me nothing.

4 Charity (love) suffereth long, and is kind; charity (love) envieth not; charity (love) vaunteth not itself, is not puffed up,

5 Doth not behave itself unseemly, seeketh not her own, is not easily provoked, thinketh no evil;

6 Rejoiceth not in iniquity, but rejoiceth in the truth;

7 Beareth all things, believeth all things, hopeth all things, endureth all things.

8 Charity (love) never faileth: but whether there be prophecies, they shall fail; whether there be tongues, they shall cease; whether there be knowledge, it shall vanish away.

9 For we know in part, and we prophesy in part.

10 But when that which is perfect is come, then that which is in part shall be done away.

11 When I was a child, I spake as a child, I understood as a child, I thought as a child: but when I became a man, I put away childish things.

12 For now we see through a glass, darkly; but then face-to-face: now I know in part; but then shall I know even as also I am known.

13 And now abideth faith, hope, charity (love), these three; but the greatest of these is charity (love).

DAY # 251   NANA'S GOODBYE

I read "Nana's Goodbye letter" and led the evening prayer for last time, tonight. I don't know how I got through it but I also read "Thank You Lord" to the group. A lot of tears and a lot of hugging followed because all thought I was going home the next day.

I read this letter to the entire dorm last night, the eve of my court date, where I would learn my fate. Everyone, including me, felt confident I would be going home.

This letter is addressed to all the ladies I've come in contact with and came to know over the last 250 days; to those who have gone the full journey with me and all the new ones that have "jumped in" along the way and those I've left behind in Rayville.

My time with you has come to an end and we must go our separate ways, but I'd like to take this opportunity to let each and every one of you know what an impact you've had on my life. Some of you I've gotten closer to than others but each of you has touched me in some way. For this I will always remember you and love you.

I'd like to share a few things I've learned over the last 8 months that might help you during your remaining time.
1.   No matter how bad your situation, there are those around you that are worse off.
2.   Be grateful for everything you've got in life (even the small things) because it can be gone in an instant.
3.   Sometimes we have to lose what we think is most dear to us to gain that which is really precious.
4.   We can learn something from everyone we meet, no matter how young or how old. Everyone comes in our lives for a reason.

5. *Sometimes God allows us to fall on our backs so we will look up.*

6. *You're never too old to start over or too young to try.*

7. *No matter how you might feel, you are never alone. God is always there to comfort you.*

The Bible reminds us to "Be not forgetful to entertain strangers, for some have entertained angels unaware." Each one of you are angels with the possibility of influencing others lives. How you influence them is up to you!

This isn't goodbye, really. Each of you has left a part of yourselves with me as I hope I have with you. Some of you I'm sure I'll see again, others I won't see until we are reunited in Heaven where there will be no locks, chains or security guards to confine us.

Until then I love each and every one of you. The Greeks had three words for love; Eros for erotic love; philos for brotherly love; and agape for Godly, unconditional love. This is the type of love I leave with you as you have given to me.

Each of you will be in my thoughts and prayers daily for you to find and live in the center of God's will everyday because then and only then will you truly be happy.

If you can remember one thing about "Old Nana" in years to come, I hope it is not just for the poems I wrote or the advice I gave, but I hope and pray you will say, "I saw Christ through her."

My Love Always,
Tracey (Nana)

NANA'S GOODBYE

It's been 250 days
And I pray my time is through,
Even though each day was spent
With wonderful friends like you.

A few are left
From when I first came.
They've been with me through every step
Of this never ending game.

First there is Julie,
Without you what would I have ever done.
Your love of life kept me going,
'Cause you knew life should be fun.

And there have been others
That stick out in my mind.
If I don't name you all
Please don't think of me as unkind.

Danielle, I so remember
When you came upon the scene.
You worried someone would steal you commissary sheet
You thought we were all so mean.

Then there is Maggie, my girl
You're a bull dog in my eye.
'Cause when you set your mind to something
You only limit is the sky.

Kim Ferris I'm really gonna miss you,
The special way you respected me.
'Cause it made me feel good about myself
That there was something special only you could see.

To the other two Kims
Ms. Tye and Ms. Lope
Your youthful inspiration and joy
Filled dismal days with hope.

And now for Sarah Cox,
You are so young my dear.
But your time for growing up
Is soon approaching, never fear.

And then there is all the rest
That I didn't get to.
But with this lump in my throat
I'm having enough trouble getting through.

You all have meant so much to me
And I love each and every one.
But Nana's time has come to an end
Her appointed time with you is done.

But don't cry because I'm leaving
Just be glad that I could go.
And if I've never told you before
You all touched my life more than you know.

No matter where you go in life
No matter what you do,
Always remember this one thing
God and Nana will always believe in you

DAY # 252   SENTENCING

Daily Blessing – *John 15:18 "If the world hate you, ye know that it hated Me before it hated you."*

I hardly slept last night thinking about all of the things I'd do when I got home; the wonderful reunion with my girls and my grandson, the food I would eat, the cokes I would drink.

I sat in the courtroom with another inmate waiting for my name to be called. I looked out across the courtroom and saw Ms. X. No surprise. Then I soon noticed someone standing behind her, patting her on the shoulder. It was my brother. I knew then that something had to be in the works that would mess up my going home.

Today I witnessed a horrible tragedy. I'm not speaking of the injustice I felt was that was dealt to me, but I saw first hand what hatred of me had done to my brother. He never looked my way but the overwhelming feeling of revulsion was so strong even those around me could feel it. The inmate that had come over to the courthouse with me made a very interesting comment. She asked what I had ever done to him that would cause him to hate me so much. I had to answer her honestly with, "I don't know."

Most inmates have family members in the gallery to support them but the only one that sat in the courtroom was there to betray me, even though I had done nothing to deserve his betrayal. I truly understand now what Shakespeare's, Jules Caesar, meant when he said as he succumbed to stab wounds by his assassin's--Mark Antony's blow. "This was the most unkind cut of all."

I didn't have long to wait before I was called to the judge's bench. He commented that he was impressed by how well my PSI looked but that he had read the victim's statement and he had received a letter from someone "very close" to me that said I had been doing this kind of thing, "ripping people off, all my life," but was just *too smart* to get caught.

My mouth literally dropped open. I knew the letter had to be from my brother, but close? We had hardly spoken in twenty-five years. How could someone not even associated with the case make a statement and that statement be believed without any proof? I was never given the opportunity to see the letter or hear its contents, let alone dispute the allegations.

The judge then issued my sentence of ten years for each of the three counts to be served concurrently with seven years suspended. That meant I was sentenced to three years. I had heard the other inmates talking about their own sentences and learned a little. I would have to serve half of that but should be eligible for early parole at one-third of the time. Either way, I wasn't going home any time soon.

There is no way I can express the betrayal I felt. I have to admit that what he had done occupied my mind more than the time I had been given. I think that I knew deep inside that my prison sentence would end, one day, but the all-consuming hatred that my brother felt toward me was a prison he would never escape. I didn't hate him for what he had done because in spite of everything that had happened, I still loved my brother.

Whether he realized it or not, God used him to teach me a valuable lesson; the consequences of hate. *Hate will rob you of happiness, hate will make you miserable, and hate will harm you physically.*

The most important consequence of hate is that hate and hell dwell in the same heart. In Galatians 5:19-21, Paul lists the works of the flesh and hate is one of them. He then goes on to say *"That they which do such things shall not inherit the kingdom of God."*

All I can do now is pray for strength to get through whatever time I have left to face and for he to come to some resolution and one day find peace with God.

I HAVE BEEN BETRAYED

I have been betrayed
By those I once held dear.
And the hurt and the anguish
Will be hard to forget I fear.

But the one that betrayed me most
Had such hatred in his eyes.
It made me see that hatred
Destroys the hater, as part of him dies.

For hatred is an emotion
That God's love cannot get through.
His commandment was to forgive one another
Even as He has forgiven you.

There is one thing the Lord has shown me
And this for my course I will set
The best form of revenge for hatred
Is merely to forgive and forget.

* The answer to my quandary about my brother didn't come until after I had gotten home. One of his long time friends told me that my own brother had hated and resented me ever since I was a child. In a way it was a relief that is wasn't anything caused by

something I had done to him. It was just sad that he had to live with the cancer of hate eating at him for so long.

DAY # 254   BETRAYAL

I felt it was time to pull out my book on I Corinthians 13 again. As I read through it, once more I was reminded of that young preacher. *What I failed to mention was the same young preacher that through sermon tried to teach me the meaning of God's love was the same one that showed up in the courtroom full of man's hatred.* What had happened in those 50 years to change him so is something I don't think I'll ever know but I still pray daily that God will touch his heart and give him some sense of peace. I also pray that God will keep my hurt from turning into hate or resentment. This is something that He and I will have to work on daily, not only towards my brother but also many others.

As I pondered and prayed over the events of yesterday the Lord put the following poem on my heart.

LOOK UP!

How do you find sanity
In an insane place?
How do you find order
When chaos fills every space?

How do you find relief
When all around you is pain?
How do you find hope
To pick up the pieces and start again?

Never fret my friend,
There is an end to your worries and fears.
There is Someone who will sustain you
Who's been there all through the years.

For God's love and power
Can fill up Heaven's skies.
But first you must look up to Him
So He can dry the tears from your eyes.

DAY # 259   SUICIDE ATTEMPT

Today, one of the younger inmates tried to slice her wrist open. She is only seventeen years old. Her attempt at a "permanent solution for a temporary situation" was brought on when her mother told her that she wouldn't help her.

What totally appalled me was the reaction of some of the other prisoners. A few were concerned with the girl's dilemma, but most of the inmates were upset because she had broken open a disposable shaver and used the blade inside. The main comment I heard was, "Well, she just caused us to lose our razors."

Does prison take away all of one's sensitivity toward your fellow man or is this just a common attitude in the world today?

MY HEAVENLY FATHER

When I need someone to pick me up
Whenever I fall down
I can always look to my Heavenly Father
For He's always around.

When I need someone to hold me up
Whenever I am tired and weak
I look to my Heavenly Father
His strength is what I seek.

When I need someone to lift me up
Whenever my spirits get low,
I look to my Heavenly Father
For I know He loves me so.

Tracey Brown

And then one day He'll raise me up
When my work on earth is through.
He'll give me a heavenly body
And all things will be made new.

Day # 262   **I Screwed Up, Lord**

Daily Blessing – *Colossians 4:2 "Continue in prayer, and watch in the same with thanksgiving"*

Today was one of those days that everything seemed to go wrong. To start off, I lost my ID badge somewhere in the dorm. Then, I sat on my glasses again and broke the other temple and I ended my day by spilling a whole cup of coffee (gold around here.) When I stopped to look over what had happened I realized I hadn't stopped this morning to do my prayer and Bible readings. There was only one way to express it.

I REALLY SCREWED UP, LORD

I really screwed things up, Lord
Theres nothing more I can say.
I didn't ask you to guide me
At the start of this new day.

I tried to go it alone
Without your guiding hand.
So, the mess I got myself into
Isn't hard to understand.

Things go so much better
When I start the day and pray.
"Dear Lord, guide my steps and thoughts"
"All through out this day."

"Keep my feet on the straight path"
"Help me keep my mind on You."
"Please let me live today"
"So others will see You in all I do."

But I was in a hurry, Lord,
As I started our today
And I forgot You and my prayers
Somewhere along the way.

Now my life is in shambles
Over something I did wrong.
My biggest mistake, dear Lord,
I didn't ask you along.

Now, I must come to You,
And ask for forgiveness, once again.
And ask that you will touch those
That I have cause so much pain.

And lastly, give me wisdom, Lord,
To know from You I should never stray.
And because I am human
I need You each and everyday.

DAY # 263   FIGHT OVER CLOTHES

Tensions were really getting high between the inmates. We had now been here for 44 days and all of that time had been spent in the dorm, right up under each other. There had been no time outside of these four walls. There was no form of recreation offered except the TV set, which only caused fights over what to watch. The books in the library had been sorted but no one had been allowed the use of the library. There had been no church groups allowed to come in to lead in any type of worship service.

This frustration was now manifesting itself between long time friends. Two of the inmates, who had been close friends on the outside, got into a fight over clothing. The guards broke the fight up just as one girl was about to bash the other girl's head on the concrete floor.

DAY # 266   JOURNEY BACK TO RPDC

Ever since I became DOC (sentenced), I felt a pull back to Rayville. I don't know if it was because of my own personal feelings or if the Lord was trying to tell me that I had unfinished work to do there.

I asked Elaine to call Warden Laing and tell her that I wanted to come back to RPDC. Warden Laing told Elaine she wanted me back but it was up to Warden Rucker of BSCF.

When Elaine called Warden Rucker, he said I wasn't going anywhere. He told her all prisons ran on numbers and he needed me as one of the numbers so that he could get the funding that he required to run the prison.

My need to leave became even more prevalent at breakfast this morning. All but one of the female guards was so busy one of the male guards helped bring in the breakfast cart. The guards at BSCF were so afraid of us that the rules stated, no less than two guards could come in the dorm and another guard had to stand watch at the interlock window. I was about fifty feet away from him but I noticed a sense of familiarity about him. I studied him for a few minutes and suddenly realized it was my nephew, Daryl. Of all of my brother's four kids I figured he was least likely to follow in his father's footsteps of being a cop.

The worst pain came when he looked straight at me and didn't even acknowledge me. This was a boy I had watched grow up, baby sat, and spent time with. After he grew up, he always seemed glad to see me when we met on the street. No matter what had transpired between my brother and me, I tried to maintain a good relationship with my nephews and niece. Had his father's lies poisoned him to the point that he couldn't acknowledge his own aunt? It seemed the curse of hatred was now becoming generational. The sins of the father were being visited upon the son.

DAY # 268   **HEADED TO A NEW MISSION FIELD**

Elaine called Warden Laing and told her what Warden Rucker had said. I don't know exactly what happened except that the hand of God intervened. I was called to the door about 10:00 this morning and told to pack my sack. I was going to Rayville.

My time in the wilderness was over and I was going back to a new mission field! Yes, my time in the wilderness was finally over. New mission field, here I come!

* I later learned that Warden Laing traded me for a prisoner that had a great deal more time left than I did. I'll always be grateful to Warden Laing and thankful to God because I don't know if things would have turned out as well as they did if I hadn't gone back.
It was hard to feel the presence of the Holy Spirit within the walls of BSCF, although I know He was there.

GLOSSARY

Blind: Area where correctional officers cannot see, as in "Let's go to the blind."

Bricks: The outside, on the outside, as in "on the bricks."

BSCF: Bossier Sheriff's Correctional Facility. The new multi-million dollar prison built in Plain Dealing, Louisiana for Bossier Parish prisoners.

Oranges: Prison clothes.

Bull Dagging: Homosexual activities between women.

Bunkie: The person with whom a prisoner shares a double bunk bed.

Call: Time for specified events -- e.g., mail call or sick call. May be known in some jurisdictions as a call out.

C.O.: Correctional Officer.

E.P.R.D.: Earliest Possible Release Date. A prisoner's release date, assuming that he or she earns credits and stays out of trouble. Computing this date can be difficult since it is based on a complex formula.

Flat Time: To serve one's time without parole.

Good Time: Credits earned toward one's sentence. In Louisiana it is usually two days for each day you serve. That means you only serve half your sentence if you keep yourself   out   of   trouble.

WHO IS DR. TRACEY BROWN?

Until November 11, 2003, Tracey Brown's 54 years on this earth had no real significance. But on that day she was arrested and spent the next 17 months in the Richland Parish Detention Center in Rayville, Louisiana.

She was raised in a Christian home and accepted Christ as her Savior at a young age. She finished college, married, and had a daughter.

Tracey Brown, PhD

With the help of a very dear friend she went back to school where she completed both her Masters and Ph.D. in Business Administration. She taught at a number of schools before opening her own consulting business.

After her best friend and business partner of 20 years died in 2002, she went into business with another female. This turned out to be what some might perceive as the biggest mistake of her life. But, praise God, He has a way of turning our biggest mistakes into our greatest triumphs.

Shortly after she arrived at RPDC the Lord showed her that she wasn't there for what she had done but for what she could do.

Although she was a Christian, she didn't have the relationship with Him that she should have. One night while alone in her cell, she surrendered every phase of her life to Him. From that day on she truly learned what it was like to walk totally by faith and not by sight.

The Lord showed her she had a talent for writing poetry. During her time behind bars the Lord placed over 400

249

poems on her heart. These poems were shared with inmates and staff alike. Many times these poems were instrumental in opening the door in witnessing to others.

Shortly after Tracey's father died, her mother turned her back on her during which time her former business partner walked away with everything she owned and wrecked havoc on her family. The Lord showed her He had so much more planned for her.

Dr. Brown's poetry has been published in numerous magazines and has recently been nominated to The International Library of Poetry's "International Who's Who in Poetry."

Dr. Brown is keeping her promise to God by helping churches and organizations set up new prison ministries and improve existing prison ministries through her work with Reach Out In Hope Ministries. Please visit their internet location at **http://www.reachoutinhope.com** for more information.